The Bat

NATURE WALK

The Bat

James V. Bradley

CHELSEA
CLUBHOUSE

An Imprint of Chelsea House Publishers

THE BAT
© 2006 by Infobase Publishing

Chelsea Clubhouse
An imprint of Infobase Publishing
132 West 31st Street
New York NY 10001

Library of Congress Cataloging-in-Publication Data

Bradley, James V. (James Vincent), 1931–
  The bat / James V. Bradley.
    p. cm. — (Nature walk)
  Includes bibliographical references and index.
  ISBN 0-7910-9117-1 (hardcover)
  1. Bats—Juvenile literature. I. Title. II. Series: Bradley, James V.
(James Vincent), 1931– Nature walk.
  QL737.C5B582 2006
  599.4—dc22   2006011763

Chelsea House books are available at special discounts when purchased in bulk quantities for businesses, associations, institutions, or sales promotions. Please call our Special Sales Department in New York at (212) 967-8800 or (800) 322-8755.

You can find Chelsea House on the World Wide Web at http://www.chelseahouse.com

TEXT AND COVER DESIGN by Takeshi Takahashi
ILLUSTRATIONS by William Bradley
SERIES EDITOR Tara Koellhoffer

Printed in the United States of America

BANG PKG 10 9 8 7 6 5 4 3 2 1

This book is printed on acid-free paper.

All links and Web addresses were checked and verified to be correct at the time of publication. Because of the dynamic nature of the Web, some addresses and links may have changed since publication and may no longer be valid.

TABLE OF CONTENTS

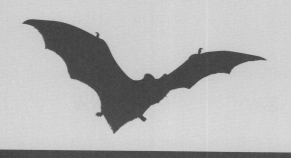

Chapter 1

Introduction to Bats

Flying Insects, Reptiles, Mammals

BATS ARE ONLY ONE KIND of flying animal. Three completely different types of animals learned to fly at different times in the distant past. The first animals to fly were insects. They were followed by flying reptiles and, much later, by flying mammals. The pterosaurs were flying reptiles that lived on Earth for over 100 million years. The smallest flying reptiles were the size of sparrows, and the largest had wingspans of 38 feet (11.6 m). Flying reptiles became extinct along with dinosaurs about

65 million years ago. Today, birds and bats are the only animals with backbones that fly.

How Did Bats Come to Fly?

Fossil bats have been found in Asia, Africa, Europe, and North and South America. The earliest fossil bats date back to about 55 million years ago. These fossil bats look much like bats do today. Bats probably originated in the Cretaceous Period during the age of dinosaurs. So far, no fossils have been found to confirm that idea. Bats probably evolved from a shrew-like insect-eating creature that lived in trees and used a membrane instead of true wings to glide from one tree to another. Changes occurred over long periods of time in the bones, muscles, and joints to allow bats to be able to fly.

Bat Anatomy and Characteristics

Bats are widespread throughout the world. They have adapted to many different environments—deserts, prairies, hardwood and coniferous forests, rain forests, and swamps. Over millions of years, the bat's **anatomy** and the functions of its parts have been shaped by the environment, especially by the food it eats. Body structures change and are refined as a species struggles to survive.

The color of a bat's fur varies by species. Bats can be gray, brown, black, pure white, rust-colored, or many different shades and combinations.

The color of a bat's fur varies by species. Some even have multicolored fur, like this fruit bat.

Some bats have truly ugly faces, with a lot of fleshy folds, spikes, bumps, and weird structures around the mouth and nostrils. These structures direct sound waves to help the bat find insects to eat. An odd-looking structure in the ear called the **targus** is used to direct echoes of sound into the bat's ear.

Many species of bats have flattened heads and rib cages. These features help them squeeze into the cracks of cave walls, where they like to roost. In contrast, the heads of bats that eat **pollen** and nectar are rounded with long cone-shaped **muzzles**.

Some bats have short, broad wings. These bats fly slowly but can turn easily in any direction. These bats are better at capturing insects in a cluttered environment, such as a jungle. Other bats have long, pointed wings. This body type lets them attack insects at a higher rate of speed. These bats are more effective in a spacious environment, such as a savanna or a prairie.

We can determine the species of a bat by looking at its teeth. The number, size, and structure of the teeth reflect the bat's feeding habits. Insect-eating bats have small, sharp, saw-like teeth, whereas vampire bats have sharp front teeth and canines and few, small molars.

The bat's tail supports a membrane that forms a pouch-like structure. It is used to capture insects. Bat ankles have a unique extension of bone called a **calcar**. Found only in bats, the calcar helps shape the pouch.

Many bats have odd or ugly faces. The strange bumps and folds on this bat's face help direct sound waves to its ears so it can catch its prey.

In one species of bat, the calcar acts like a sixth digit—something like an opposable thumb that helps the bat cling to tree branches.

There is something strange about the feet of bats. They're backwards. The lower leg, from the knee down, is rotated 180 degrees from the normal position. The knee and the bones of the lower legs are reversed, along with all of the muscles and nerves. When a bat attaches to a cave wall or the branch of a tree, it grabs the branch with its clawed toes the same way you hold a stick with both hands. It can rotate its feet the same way you can rotate your hands 180 degrees.

Some kinds of bats have flat heads and rib cages. This makes it easier for the bat to squeeze into narrow spaces, such as the crevices in the walls of caves.

CLASSIFYING BATS

All bats are mammals. They have hair and they nurse their young with **mammary glands**. Like humans, they are part of the class Mammalia. A class is a huge category that separates major animal groups, such as mammals, reptiles, amphibians, and fish. Classes are broken down into smaller categories called orders. Because bats are the only mammals that truly fly, rather than glide, they have their very own order, *Chiroptera*.

Valves in the veins of bats help prevent blood from flowing in the wrong direction. This allows bats to sleep upside down. Sleeping upside down has obvious benefits for bats. When they let go, gravity gives them the initial energy they need for takeoff. No running or flapping of the wings is needed to start flying. There is also safety in numbers, and many bats can be packed close together side-by-side on the roof of a cave or on a tree limb.

Another unique feature lets the bat hang in its sleeping position without using any energy. The bat inserts a claw into a depression or crack in a cave wall. The bat's weight then pulls down on a tendon that passes through a sheath and pulls down at the base of the claw. A lever system pulls the claw forward, and a special ratchet-like structure in the sheath locks the tendon in place. The bat can now hang securely in place without contracting any muscles. When the bat wants to break free, it contracts its leg muscles, and the tendon loosens.

Although humans are not as flexible as bats, we can take a pose close to that of the flying bat. To do this, we extend the arm over the head with the thumb pointing forward and the four fingers spread apart and pointing backward. Both the human arm and hand and the wing of a bat show the same basic pattern: There is a single bone (the humerus) for the upper arm and two bones (the radius and ulna) in the

A bat has special valves in its veins that allow it to hang and even sleep upside down without its blood flowing in the wrong direction.

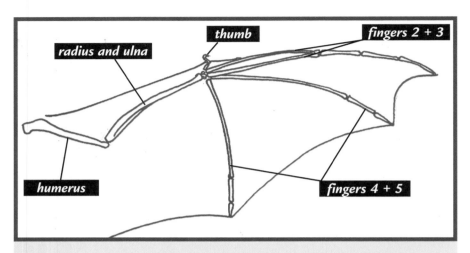

The arm of a bat follows the same basic pattern as the human arm. There is one bone (the humerus) in the upper arm, and two bones (the radius and ulna) in the lower arm, along with wrist bones (carpels) and the finger bones.

lower arm, followed by wrist bones (carpels) and five digits. Bat bones are hollow and thin, to keep the bat's weight low and help bats fly. In the bat, the ulna is fused with the radius to decrease weight even more and add strength to the wing. The thumb has a claw at the end. The other four fingers support the wing membrane. The finger bones play a minor role in absorbing some of the physical stress of flight.

Bats vary in size. The bumblebee bat is about 1.5 inches (3.8 cm) long and weighs about 2 grams (0.07 oz; less than a dime). The largest fruit bat weighs about 1.5 kg (3.3 lbs) and has a wingspan of 2 meters (over 6 feet).

Chapter 2

Bats in Myth and Culture

Myths About Bats

THERE ARE A LOT OF MYTHS and legends about bats—and most of them are false. Bats, for example, do not get tangled in human hair. Sometimes at dusk bats will circle people and appear to dive-bomb their heads. Actually, the bats are just attracted to the insects that people disturb and to the mosquitoes that we attract. When a bat makes a sharp turn, it slows down and then dives to gain speed and prevent stopping. The popular phrase "You're

17

batty" probably comes from the erratic, seemingly crazy, flight patterns of bats as they hunt insects.

The expression "blind as a bat" relates to the fact that many insect-eating bats have small eyes tucked in their thick fur. In reality, bats are not blind. Their vision is actually quite good.

Bats are not flying mice. In fact, they are not rodents at all. Rodents belong to the order Rodentia, but bats have their own order, Chiroptera, which means "hand-wing."

Bats as Part of Culture

Most cultures, ancient and modern, have something to say about bats. Bat stories often include themes

LISTENING TO BATS

It is now possible to hear the **echolocation** sounds of bats with relatively inexpensive electronic equipment. This opens up all kinds of possibilities for amateur naturalists to study bats. For example, someone could listen to both the naturally heard and **high-frequency** sounds that bats make when they are roosting. Humans hear sounds up to 20 KHz (kilohertz). Most bat species make sounds that start at around 20 KHz and go higher, and each species has its own narrow range of sounds. Detectors that can hear bat sounds are available with ranges from 10 to 120 KHz at prices that range from $100 to more than $1,000.

about good and evil, sunlight and darkness, life and death, and all the mysteries of existence.

The aborigines of Australia gave the bat a central role in their explanation of how death first made its appearance. The story is: When the first man and woman were made and placed on Earth, they were immortal and lived free of fear. Only one rule was placed upon them by their creator. They were told to stay away from a certain cave. This cave was guarded by a large bat that hung upside down in front of the cave. The bat had spiritual powers. The creator's order was very specific: Don't disturb the bat.

The woman eventually became so curious about the cave that she ignored the order. As she approached, the huge bat looked at the woman as if shocked by her approach. To the woman's surprise, the bat just flew away.

Then, as the woman watched, a dark, human-like form slowly crawled out of the cave. It was death. The bat had been holding death prisoner. Now that the bat had been disturbed, death was free. The man and the woman fled in terror. Since that time, all human beings have had to die.

Aesop's Fables: Why Bats Fly at Night

Even Aesop's fables have something to say about bats. At one time, the fables say, the birds and animals fought a war to see which of them was stronger.

Thinking it was a mixture of both bird and animal, the bat decided to wait and join the stronger side after the battle was already under way. The war started, and the birds were very tough. They appeared to be winning the war. Seeing this, the bat joined in with the birds by swinging a club and beating back the animals. After a while, the animals turned the tide of battle and eventually won the war. They were very angry at the bat and put it on trial. The court found the bat guilty of deserting the animals. As punishment, the bat was condemned to a life of darkness, never to see the sun again.

Chapter 3

Bats and the Night Life

Why Bats Fly at Night—A Scientific Explanation

BATS ARE **nocturnal** in their feeding habits. That is, they feed mainly at night. Occasionally, bats are seen flying in the daylight, but this is usually because they have been disturbed in some way. Scientific research points to three reasons why bats became nocturnal feeders: 1) Hunting at night would help bats avoid birds of prey that might kill them; 2) Nighttime hunting lets bats avoid competing with birds for the same foods; 3) Bats

Most bats fly mainly at night. If you see a bat flying during daylight hours, it has most likely been bothered in some way.

have trouble handling heat so flying during the day, when temperatures are warmer, could cause them to overheat and die.

All three reasons make sense, but they can't account for why bats hunt at night in so many different environments. For example, there are many islands on which bats live that don't have any birds of prey, but even there, bat populations are nocturnal. Bats in the tropics are pretty much limited to nocturnal hunting because of the intense heat during the day. Bats in temperate climates, on the other hand, have many opportunities to hunt the many summer insects in the early morning and late afternoon when temperatures are cool, but they do not take advantage of this easy source of food. Cases like these have made scientists admit that they don't completely understand why bats do not change their habits, even when doing so could give them an obvious advantage for survival.

How Do Bats Catch Flying Insects?

Some bats catch insects by picking them off plants or off the ground, but most bats catch insects in flight. Bats use a method of finding objects by using sound waves to catch insects and avoid obstacles when flying in the dark. The method is called echolocation. As the bat hunts, it lets off high-frequency sounds through its mouth or nose, depending on the species. These sounds are too high-pitched for humans to hear. When the sound waves strike an insect or other object, they echo back to the bat, and the bat interprets them. Echolocation is so effective that experiments done in complete darkness show that bats can even avoid running into very thin threads that are hung from the ceiling.

High-frequency sound waves can travel far in open spaces such as prairies. Lower frequencies carry farther in cluttered spaces, such as dense forests. It is therefore reasonable to assume that the bats that skim over the tops of grasses in prairies would let off higher-frequency sounds than bats that hunt in dense tropical forests. That is exactly what happens.

How Bats Hunt

At first, the bat hunts in search mode, giving off lower-frequency sound waves. When it detects an insect, its ears and head turn toward the prey. It then switches to an approach mode, increasing the frequency of the sounds it makes to pinpoint the location of the insect. The bat's brain has to be able to tell the difference between the insect and background noise, since sound waves bounce back from all nearby objects—leaves, branches, tree trunks, flying birds, and insects other than the one being targeted.

If the insect is a slow flyer, the bat heads directly toward it and catches it. With a fast-moving insect that makes sharp, quick movements, such as a moth, a bat will often change its course and approach the insect from the rear. Once the insect is "locked in" to the bat's **sonar**, the bat tries to keep the angle of flight between the insect and itself constant to predict the insect's flight path. This is quite a job, considering all the twists, dives, and sharp turns that take place

AN EASIER METHOD OF HUNTING

In nature, time management rules. If an animal spends more energy capturing food than it gets from eating the food, it is in trouble. The bat *Hipposideros speoris* has come up with a hunting technique that gives it an edge. Rather than fly after insects, these bats wait for insects to come to them. When the hunt starts, they go to a favorite site—perhaps in a swamp or along a riverbank—and hang from a favorite tree. Then they give off sound waves to detect any insects that come within striking range, which is anywhere from 7 to 36 meters (7.7 to 39 yards). The bat then darts out, captures the insects, and returns to its hiding spot—all within about four seconds. The bats only fly to capture insects, not to find them.

during the chase. The chase takes only a matter of seconds, even milliseconds, rather than minutes. One study placed the average number of insects caught by bats at seven per minute.

In the final milliseconds before capturing its prey, the bat usually reduces its speed and lets out one last burst of sound. This is another time where the bat's reversed legs become useful: The bat brings its legs and rear end forward under its wings, creating a pouch-like structure with the skin between the two legs and the tail. The bat catches the insect in its pouch and then dips its head into the pouch to grab the insect with its mouth. As they do this, some bats will make a complete somersault. The insect is usually eaten in flight and its wings thrown away. As far as we know, bats do not catch insects in their mouths in flight, but sometimes they will capture them in their wings.

A Moth Under Attack Fights Back

Scientists learned about how bats capture insects and how insects avoid capture by putting photography together with sound recordings. This enables them to see, for example, how a moth will try to escape from a hunting bat. Once a bat "locks in" on a moth, capture is not necessarily a sure thing. A moth may avoid being caught by making a last-second movement. After a miss, the bat may circle and make another try. More likely, it will look for another prey.

If the use of sonar to find prey is amazing, the use of sonar to avoid being caught is even more wonderful. The brain of an insect is not at all as complex as the brain of a bat, and yet the moth has developed a way to mess up echolocation. Some moths can detect a bat's sonar by using the oval-shaped eardrum it has on each side of its body. When it realizes a bat is near, the moth tries to confuse the bat by making highly erratic turns and diving into protective vegetation. Some moths can produce high-frequency sounds that "jam" the bat's sonar. The sounds the moths make are similar to the echoes the bat receives when the moth is close enough to be caught. The bat responds to the false data by forming a pouch to capture a moth that is not there. Then the moth escapes. Through the process of **natural selection**, some bat species have raised the frequency of the sounds they make above the range that can be heard by moths, thus ruining the moth's defense.

Chapter 4

Kinds of Bats

Microbats and Megabats

There are more than 950 species of bats, and they live on every continent except Antarctica. All bats belong to the order Chiroptera and form two groups or suborders: microbats (microchiroptera) and megabats (megachiroptera).

Microbats are most numerous and are found throughout the world. They are usually small, and most of them are insect eaters. Some also include fruit, **nectar**, and flowers in their diet, while others are strict vegetarians.

These bats are important because they help spread pollen and seeds for many trees and plants, which helps these types of vegetation reproduce.

Megabats are sometimes referred to as "Old World bats." They are large and come from Southeast Asia, India, Africa, and Australia. They are sometimes called flying foxes and feed entirely on fruits, flowers, and nectar. Megabats are handsome animals. Their faces show their intelligence, curiosity, and individuality. Some megabats have a wingspan of over 6 feet (1.8 m). All nine species of megabats face some kind of threat; some are **endangered** because their habitat is being destroyed, most often by humans.

Fossils show that microbats have lived on Earth for at least 55 million years. Megabats are believed to have evolved from a branch of microbats around 35 million years ago. Some scientists claim that megabats are not related to microbats at all but evolved instead from an early primate. These scientists point to similarities in brain structures and other evidence for support. **DNA** comparisons, however, favor the idea that both megabats and microbats had a single common ancestor.

A Variety of Species
LONG-NOSED BAT
The long-nosed bat is found in the deserts of New Mexico, Arizona, and Mexico. It eats nectar and fruit

Megabats are the group of larger bats. Some megabats have a wingspan of over 6 feet (1.8 m).

from the giant cactus and other plants. As it eats nectar, the bat's fur gets coated with pollen. If the bats did not help spread this pollen, much of the desert **ecology** would be very different.

HAIRY-LEGGED VAMPIRE

This bat from Mexico is rather attractive. It has large eyes and lacks deep nose folds. It feeds more often on birds than on mammals, and attacks birds as they roost in trees at night. The hairy-legged vampire bat's canine teeth have adapted to puncture thin bird skin. Because of this, the wounds it makes are not as deep as those made by vampire bats that feed on the blood of mammals. The birds are not harmed by the process of feeding.

SWORD-NOSED BATS

There are several species of sword-nosed bats, and they're all ugly. These bats live in the dense forests of Mexico. They create sound through their nose, and a spear-like structure on the nose directs the sound toward prey. The bats also have long, bushy structures in front of the ears, which may further help direct echoes to the ear.

LINNAEUS'S FALSE VAMPIRE

These "false" vampire bats are among the largest microbats. Scientists once believed that these bats

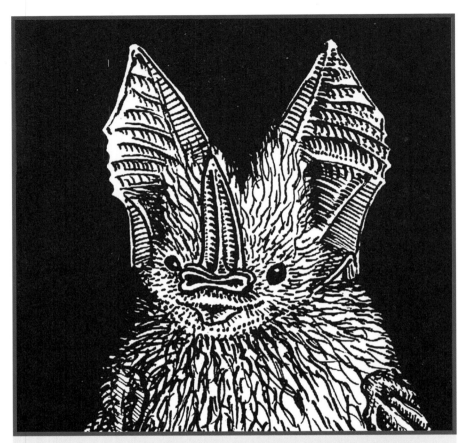

Sword-nosed bats have a strange spear-shaped structure on their nose. It helps direct sound waves toward the bat's prey.

drink blood, but they don't, which gives them the name "false vampire." The false vampires capture their prey by picking up small animals—such as mice, insects, and birds—from plants or the ground. They find their prey both by echolocation and by listening for the sounds the prey makes.

Big Brown Bat

This bat is found in Canada, throughout the United States, and in Mexico. If you have a large **colony** of bats in your attic, the chances are good that it's a colony of big browns. These bats can often be seen flitting around street lamps in towns and cities as they search for insects. The attic-loving little brown bat is a champion mosquito hunter. These bats are found mainly in the northern two-thirds of the United States and in Canada.

Mexican Free-tailed Bat

There are six species of free-tailed bats in the United States. Mexican free-tailed bats are the most numerous cave-roosting bats in the United States. From March through October, you can witness the emergence of hundreds of thousands of bats each evening from Bracken Cave near San Antonio, Texas.

Fish-eating Bats

A fishing bat of Mexico, called the *Noctilio leporinus*, is found in the semitropical and tropical regions of the Americas. This bat flies low over bodies of fresh water, extending its long legs to drag their oversized, sharply clawed feet through the water. The bat uses echolocation to detect any ripples caused by an exposed fish fin on the surface of the water. Its sharp claws close tightly on any fish they touch. Sometimes

Big brown bats are very common throughout the United States, Canada, and Mexico.

the bat eats the fish in flight; other times it brings the fish to a nearby roost to eat it.

BIRD-EATING BAT

Spanish scientists published a paper in the National Academy of Sciences in 2001. It said that an insect-eating bat called the greater noctule bat also feeds on small birds. This bat is reddish in color and can have a wingspan of 18 inches (46 cm). Feathers found in waste products confirmed that the bats were eating small birds that **migrate** across the Mediterranean Sea.

BLOOD-EATING BATS

Vampire bats are relatively small. They have a wingspan of about 30 cm (about 12 inches). They weigh about 1 ounce (28 g) and they make little or no noise as they approach their prey. Unlike other bat species, they have strong legs that let them hop and scramble over surfaces. They can also jump straight up to take flight.

After landing close to a victim, they move closer to get into position. They have two pointed, razor-sharp front teeth and two canines that slice a V-shaped wedge, about the size of a pinhead, through the skin. They seem to prefer to feast on toes, but will feed at any place with a good supply of blood, such as the tip of the nose, ear, or lips. The cut they make is so clean and small that most people sleep right through it.

The bat laps at the blood with its tongue, which contains tiny grooves that carry the blood into the mouth. The saliva contains an **anticoagulant** that prevents the blood from clotting and drying.

A vampire bat needs to consume 57 percent of its weight in blood each day to survive—that's about 15 to 30 ml (1 tablespoon) of blood. It can get this much blood at one good meal that lasts about 20 minutes. After the meal, the small wound on the victim continues to bleed for quite a long time, and the victim usually wakes up with a bloody mess.

Populations of vampire bats are concentrated in southern Mexico and Central and South America. They are the only mammals that feed on blood alone, and they get their blood by biting their prey. There are only three living species of vampire bats. One of these—the hairy-legged vampire, *Diphylla*—feeds mainly on the blood of birds. Another—the white-winged bat, *Diaemus*—can eat mammal blood, but it must drink bird blood at least once a week or it will die. The common vampire bat, called *Desmodus rotundus*, is more closely associated with feeding on humans. Even so, these bats feed more often on cattle, horses, and other farm mammals. With more land being used for cattle-rearing in South America, the *Desmodus* population has exploded and its range has spread into the more temperate climate of northern Mexico. These bats have been seen in some southern border towns in Texas.

A vampire bat with rabies is a threat to humans because of its unique habit of biting. Getting rabies from an ordinary insect-eating bat is possible, but this is relatively rare and usually happens when a person handles a sick bat.

How Did the Method of Feeding on Blood Evolve?

Getting nutrition by drinking blood is really not very different from eating the muscle tissue, bones, and other organs of an entire animal. It is, however, a challenge to explain the vampire bat's specialized form of feeding.

It is possible that the first **protovampires**—those bats that later evolved into vampire bats—got their first exposure to blood by feeding on ticks that were attached to the skin of mammals. These bats would have had sharp teeth, just as insect-eating bats do today. It seems to be an easy step to start slicing into the skin to get at the blood more directly. Feeding on fly **larvae** on open wounds is another way that protovampires might have begun to feed on blood.

Chapter 5

Bats and People

Rabies and Bats

Getting people to accept bats into their community sounds odd, considering people's fear of rabies. Rabies is a deadly disease that attacks the central nervous system and, once symptoms occur, it is often fatal. Only about one person in the United States dies each year of rabies transmitted by bats, but the threat of rabies is always present and safety measures should be taken in advance. Bat bites usually result from handling sick or disabled bats or from accidental encounters in which a bat feels threatened. Here are some facts about rabies and bats:

- Bats do not get rabies more often than any other wild mammal, such as skunks and raccoons.
- Bats do not have rabies and remain healthy. If they have the disease, they are actively sick.
- Bats, even sick bats, are rarely aggressive, but they will bite if they feel threatened.
- The rabies **virus** has not been found in the feces or urine of bats. Rabies is spread by contact with the bat's saliva, usually through a bite or scratch.
- When bats do contract rabies, they die rather quickly.

To avoid the danger of rabies, never approach a bat that is on the ground or one that appears weak. Because they are so curious, small children should be warned against approaching such a bat. If physical contact is made with a bat, the bat should be captured for safety tests.

A Good Response to Bats

What would your reaction be if bats started using a bridge in your city as a favorite roosting site? What if there were hundreds at first, then thousands, then tens of thousands of bats within the city limits? What about the threat of rabies? What about the bats' urine and fecal waste? What about the spread of disease? The typical response of most people would be to drive the bats away or, if that didn't work, to kill them.

This kind of bat problem struck the Congress Avenue Bridge in Austin, Texas, in the early 1980s. After much discussion, the people of Austin finally decided to accept and live with the bats. One of the advantages of having 1.5 million Mexican free-tailed bats living close by is that they eat 10 to 15 tons (9 to 13.6 metric tons) of insects every night. Austin is now called the "Bat Capital of the World," and the bridge where the bats roost is a major tourist attraction. There have been no cases of bat-transmitted rabies in humans in Austin.

Chapter 6

Where Bats Live

Roosting in Caves and Other Places

Caves and abandoned mines are ideal homes, or roosts, for bats because the temperature and humidity don't vary much. Remember how small these creatures are. Any major change in body heat can be deadly.

Some caves are year-round roosts that house millions of bats. The bats leave the caves in the evening and return before morning. Other species spend the summer in the Canadian tundra feeding on insects, and then migrate south to spend the winter in Mexico.

Many bats roost in caves all year long. They leave the cave at night to hunt and return in the morning before the sun comes up.

Many species in warm climates migrate to caves each year to **hibernate** during the winter and to raise their young in the spring. These bats spend most of the year at feeding grounds far away from caves. They roost in small groups in trees, under rocks, in attics, under cliff edges, in woodpiles, squeezed under the loose bark of trees, and many other places. If caves are available, however, bats will use them. Some bats,

A MODERN SUBSTITUTE FOR CAVES

Bat populations have suffered from the loss of habitat and the prejudice of humans. Many species are now threatened. In an effort to boost bat populations and prevent extinction, the organization Bat Conservation International (BCI) has found an excellent substitute for caves in the thousands of highway bridges throughout the country. Working with state highway departments and guidance from BCI, volunteers have built and installed bat houses under bridges in many states, especially in the South. Many states, cities and suburban and farm communities have problems with insects. Bats make excellent "insect vacuum machines" and reduce the need for **pesticides**.

You can buy bat houses like these to welcome bats to your own backyard.

such as the little brown bat and the big brown bat, prefer to roost in houses and other buildings.

Bats will leave their favorite roosts in search of
food and live for the summer in different locations.
Since bats are nocturnal, they usually avoid occupied
buildings, preferring quieter places such as deserted
factories, barns, and houses. They will also roost in
the attics of residential homes and, in most cases,

**Some species of bats roost on leaves, among other
unusual places.**

will not be noticed. Some species prefer to roost in trees and bushes, hollow logs, and outcrops of rock or under stones.

Hanging from the ceiling of a cave is one of safest places in the world for a bat—think of a carpet of bats on the ceiling of a deep, dark cave. There is safety in numbers. If a predator wanders nearby, the bats sound an alarm and quickly leave the area. Bats have many predators, but only the rat makes a habit of going deep into mineshafts or caves for a meal.

More Exotic Roosting Places

Several species of African bats live on the young curled leaves of banana plants. Some have special button-like structures at the base of their thumbs that prevent them from slipping. Other bat species in Mexico and South America also use banana leaves this way.

The lesser-footed club bat uses the opening chewed into bamboo stalks by insects to get inside a section of bamboo, which it uses as a snug roosting place. This is one species of bat that does not roost upside down.

The Seminole bat roosts in the Spanish moss that hangs from many trees throughout the southeastern United States. The Spanish moss offers shade, an occasional cool breeze, and an excellent hiding place that is high off the ground and away from predators.

The white bat is a fruit-eating bat found in Honduras and farther south down to Panama. It builds a temporary shelter by cutting the side veins of the Heliconia leaf. This makes the sides of the leaf fold down to form a tent, which provides shelter from rain and sun and also hides the bats from predators.

The Bat Lifestyle

Bats as Both Predator and Prey

A huge mass of bats can be seen every evening, just when the light is fading, at Carlsbad Caverns, New Mexico. That's when millions of bats leave the caves in their nighttime search for insects. From a mile or two away, the bats look like a funnel of black smoke leaving the ground and fanning out over a broad area. Together, the bats are probably the most effective, simplest insect-control machine on Earth.

When the bats leave the cave, they can easily be attacked by predators. Hawks gather each evening and

When bats leave their roosts to hunt, they often move in large groups. This helps protect the individual bats from predators, since it's hard to capture a single bat in a swarm of hundreds or thousands.

wait for the chance to pick off a bat for an easy meal. The bats counter this danger by leaving the cave in massive numbers in a flurry of flying and loud chirping. Picking out one individual bat is not so easy. One interesting observation is that the bats could avoid these hawks just by waiting a few more minutes before leaving the cave, when the light is too dim for the hawks to hunt. They don't do this, however, probably because the few bats that are lost don't affect the strength of the bat colony as a whole.

Snakes and raccoons are also waiting when the bats fly away from their cave. The temptation is too great to let an invitation to so much protein go to waste. A snake will lie coiled on a favorite branch close to the cave exit while raccoons wait to jump into the mass of bats. As the bats come out, the snake just has to wait for one to fly within reach. Then it strikes and gets its evening meal.

Mating Time

Each species of bat has its own reproductive story, and sometimes the stories differ a lot. In general, male and female bats hunt and roost together through most of the year. In the fall, the male searches for mates. In some species, a male keeps a **harem** of several females and defends his territory during the mating period.

In the spring, a pregnant bat will leave her hibernation cave and return to the cave where she was born. This cave serves as a nursery. The males roost in another area of the cave or at another site. In most species, the male bats take no interest in the offspring.

The mother usually gives birth to only one infant or, on occasion, twins. In some species, the mother gives birth while hanging upside down; in others, she assumes a horizontal position.

The infant is born pink, hairless, and with its eyes closed. Claws on its wings and toes enable the tiny bat to climb down the mother's body to reach the mammary glands. The baby bat uses its special sharply curved teeth to attach to get milk. The combination of teeth and claws anchors the baby securely to the mother's chest, even in flight.

Caring for the Young

During the first week of her baby's life, the mother helps the baby attach its claws and feet to the cave wall. She carries the infant even while hunting insects.

In three to four days, the baby's eyes open and hair begins in grow. As the young bat's weight increases, it is left behind in the cave at night while the mother hunts. The young bats in the cave crawl over the rock surface and gather in clusters to keep warm. Sometimes the clusters are so huge that the wall looks like a carpet. When the mother returns, she finds her

Young bats roost on the walls of caves, and remain there while their mothers go out to hunt.

infant among the masses of bodies in total darkness by listening for its distinct call. At closer range, the infant's odor also helps the mother identify it. The infant climbs onto the mother to nurse. Bats make as many as three or four trips to the cave each night to nurse their young. Nursing continues for three to four weeks—and in some species for more than seven weeks—even while the young are learning to catch insects.

During their time in the cave, the young bats develop a complex system of calls that include the high-frequency echolocation calls. In fact, echolocation might have its origins in mother-offspring bond-

Most species of bats continue to nurse for three to four weeks after they are born.

ing. Special echolocation calls are also developed at this time so that individuals can recognize members of their own colony. This type of vocal identification helps members of a group recognize one another and return again and again to specific roosting, hibernation, and maternity sites.

In about two to six weeks, depending on the species, the young bats take their first flight in complete darkness without bumping into anything. It is now that the bats learn how to use echolocation, first with short flights, then with longer ones. Their brains develop "sight" though echolocation first and later through visual means when they leave the cave. Soon the ability to move smoothly and quickly improves enough for the juveniles to leave the cave and learn to hunt with the adults. However, during this learning period, the young bats continue to nurse until they can catch their own food. Once they can hunt for themselves, they are on their own, and the mother can join the other adult males and females until the next breeding season.

Community Cooperation

Bat mothers and their infants form a community of cooperation. At dusk, the mothers leave to hunt, but a few adult females will remain behind to watch over the young bats. If an infant falls to the cave floor, the "babysitter" will pick up the infant and return it to the cluster. If an infant is left unfed or is orphaned, nearby females will **instinctively** nurture and rear it. This instinct is an important mechanism for the survival of the colony, since the birth rate of only one offspring per year is so low. Some species practice **communal feeding**—females feed any baby that is hungry.

Torpor and Hibernation

Bats have to keep their internal body temperature constant, just as humans do. In hot weather the bat

Young bats take their first flight two to six weeks after they are born, but they continue to roost in the same cave as their mothers and will nurse until they are capable of hunting for themselves. After that, they are on their own.

cools itself by panting, seeking out cool places, not flying, spreading its wings to increase surface area for cooling, and licking or urinating on itself. In severe cases, bats can enter a state of **torpor**—a lethargic, sleepy, low-energy state where body functions that create heat, such as muscle activity and digestion, decrease. Bats also enter a state of torpor to deal with temporary changes in the environment, such as a sudden loss of insects due to a drought or a sudden, short cold spell.

Hibernation is a deeper form of torpor. A bat that is disturbed even once during hibernation uses up a large amount of its stored fat and may not be able to survive the winter. It is important to leave bats alone in the wild, for their protection and your own.

anatomy—The structure of the body of a living thing.

anticoagulant—A substance that prevents blood from clotting and drying.

calcar—An extension of bone that helps a bat form a pouch.

colony—A large group of bats that live together in one place.

communal feeding—A system in which female bats will feed the offspring of other females for the good of the whole colony.

DNA—Deoxyribonucleic acid; nucleic acids that make up the genes that are responsible for passing traits from parents to their offspring.

echolocation—A process that uses sound waves to locate objects that cannot be seen.

ecology—The relationships between living things and their environment.

endangered—Threatened with extinction.

harem—A group of females associated with a single male.

hibernate—Pass the winter in a resting state.

high-frequency—Referring to sound waves that measure toward the high end of a radio frequency scale.

instinctively—Prompted by a natural response to a particular situation.

larvae—Young, worm-like baby insects.

mammary glands—Glands in female mammals that secrete milk.

migrate—Move to a different location with the change of seasons.

muzzles—Snouts.

natural selection—A process by which those animals that are best adapted to their environment survive to reproduce.

nectar—A sweet liquid secreted by plants.

nocturnal—Active at night.

pesticides—Chemicals used to kill insects.

pollen—Material found in seed plants that looks like fine dust. When spread to other plants, pollen allows for plant reproduction.

protovampire—Early form of a vampire bat.

sonar—A method of detecting objects by using sound waves.

targus—A structure in the ear of a bat that helps direct sound waves into the ear.

torpor—A state of mental and muscular inactivity.

virus—An extremely simple microorganism that needs to be inside a living cell in order to reproduce. Some viruses cause disease.

BIBLIOGRAPHY

Fenton, M. Brock. "Wounds and the Origin of Blood-feeding in Bats." *Biological Journal of the Linnaean Society* 47 (1992): 161–171.

Hill, John E., and James D. Smith. *Bats: A Natural History*. Austin: University of Texas Press, 1984.

Pearl, D. L., and M. B. Fenton. "Can Echolocation Calls Provide Information About Group Identity in the Little Brown Bat (*Myotis lucifugus*)?" *Canada Journal of Zoology* 74 (1996): 2184–2192.

Racy, Paul A., and Susan M. Swift, eds. *Ecology, Evolution and Behavior of Bats*. New York: Oxford Science Publications, 1995.

Roeder, K. D., and A. E. Treat. "The Detection and Evasion of Bats by Moths." *Smithsonian Report* (1961) 455–464.

Speakerman, John R. "Chiropteran Nocturnality." *Journal of Zoology* 67 (1995): 187–201.

Tuttle, Merlin D. "The Amazing Frog-Eating Bat." *National Geographic* 161 (1) (1986): 78–90.

Graham, Gary L. *Bats of the World*. New York: St. Martin's Press, 2001.

Hall, Leslie, and Greg Richards. *Flying Foxes: Fruit and Blossom Bats of Australia*. Melbourne, Australia: Krieger Publishing Company, 2001.

Tuttle, Merlin D. *America's Neighborhood Bats: Understanding and Learning to Live in Harmony with Them*. Austin: University of Texas Press, 2005.

Williams, Kim, Rob Mies, Donald Stokes, and Lillian Stokes. *Stokes Beginner's Guide to Bats*. Little, Brown, 2002.

Web Sites

Bat Conservation International
  www.batcon.org

Lubee Foundation
  www.lubee.org

Organization for Bat Conservation
  www.batconservation.org

ABOUT THE AUTHOR

James V. Bradley taught biology at Lake Forest High School in Lake Forest, Illinois, for 25 years. He also taught science in Colorado and in the United Kingdom. Bradley received the Illinois STAR Award (Science Teaching Achievement Recognition) in 1980 and was named by the National Association of Biology Teachers as outstanding biology teacher in Illinois in 1981. He retired from teaching in 1994, but continues to write and study science topics.

RODALE ORGANIC **GARDENING BASICS**

vegetables

D1445006

RODALE

**From the Editors of
Rodale Organic Gardening
Magazine and Books**

RODALE

WE **INSPIRE** AND **ENABLE** PEOPLE TO IMPROVE
THEIR LIVES AND THE WORLD AROUND THEM

© 2000 by Rodale Inc.

We're always happy to hear from you. For questions or comments concerning the editorial content of this book, please write to:

Rodale Book Readers' Service
33 East Minor Street
Emmaus, PA 18098

Look for other Rodale books wherever books are sold. Or call us at (800) 848-4735.

For more information about Rodale Organic Gardening magazine and books, visit us at:

www.organicgardening.com

Editor: Christine Bucks
Interior Book Designer: Nancy Smola Biltcliff
Cover Designer: Patricia Field
Photography Editor: Lyn Horst
Layout Designer: Dale Mack
Researchers: Celia Cameron, Sarah Wolfgang Heffner, Pamela A. Ruch, and Heidi A. Stonehill
Copy Editors: Christine Bucher and Erana Bumbardatore
Manufacturing Coordinator: Mark Krahforst
Indexer: Nan Badgett
Editorial Assistance: Kerrie A. Cadden

RODALE ORGANIC GARDENING BOOKS
Managing Editor: Fern Marshall Bradley
Executive Creative Director: Christin Gangi
Art Director: Patricia Field
Production Manager: Robert V. Anderson Jr.
Studio Manager: Leslie M. Keefe
Associate Copy Manager: Jennifer Hornsby
Manufacturing Manager: Mark Krahforst

**Library of Congress
Cataloging-in-Publication Data**
Rodale organic gardening basics.
Vegetables / from the editors of Rodale Organic Gardening Magazine and Books.
        p.   cm.
    Includes bibliographical references (p.   ) and index.
    ISBN 0-87596-840-6 (pbk. : alk. paper)
    1. Vegetable gardening.   2. Organic gardening.   I. Rodale Books.
SB324.3 .O738   2000
635'.0484—dc21   99-050444

Distributed in the book trade by St. Martin's Press

2   4   6   8   10   9   7   5   3   1   paperback

contents

The Joy of Organic Vegetable Gardening

Once you've eaten a fresh organic vegetable right out of your garden, it's difficult to go back to eating anything else. You can taste the life in it, still sweet from the sun.

From the first tender lettuces of spring to summer's bounty of tomatoes, peppers, and beans, right on through the final squash and pumpkins of fall, there's nothing more satisfying than eating food fresh from the garden.

More than ever, though, it's essential to grow your vegetables organically. Dozens of scientific studies have shown the connection between chemical pesticides and fertilizers and human health—whether it's a link to cancer, hormonal imbalances, or even neurological damage (especially in the case of pesticides). These days, there's simply no good reason to use chemicals in your home garden.

And if you have children, growing vegetables organically is even more crucial because even very low levels of pesticide residues (which adults might be able to tolerate) can be toxic to our little ones. I absolutely love going out to my organic garden with my children to check "what's for dinner." Seeing my two-year-old enjoying fresh fava beans and cherry tomatoes right from the vine is a true joy!

I've been growing vegetables organically for 20 years with minimum effort and maximum harvest. This book is all you need to get started on the organic gardener's path to delicious, nutritious, and life-filled vegetable growing (and eating!).

Happy organic gardening!

Maria Rodale

Maria Rodale

Once you've eaten a freshly grown organic vegetable right out of your garden, it's difficult to go back to eating anything else.

Growing vegetables the organic way can be less time-consuming than and just as bountiful as growing them with chemicals.

Go Organic: Vegetable Gardening Simplified

One of the great joys of vegetable gardening is picking a ripe pea pod or cherry tomato off the vine and eating it—right there in the garden. And that's one great reason to make your vegetable garden organic: You'll never have to worry about whether there are chemicals in or on what you harvest.

Gardening organically can also make your gardening routine simpler and less time-consuming. In an organic garden, there's a natural balance between the soil, crops, insects, and other animals. The soil feeds the plants, and the plants are so naturally healthy that they resist harm from most pest insects or diseases. Plus, your organic garden will be full of helpful insects and other creatures that help build soil and fight pests: Earthworms, lady beetles, birds, and toads are just a few examples of the "good guys" (also known as beneficials) that you may find in and around your garden.

With such healthy plants and so many helpers, you'll find you spend little time worrying about fertilizing and controlling pests. And that means you'll have more time to spend enjoying and relaxing in your garden.

In an organic garden, there's a natural balance between the soil, crops, insects, and other animals.

10 THINGS YOU CAN STOP DOING NOW

If you're already a vegetable gardener (or if you've tried growing vegetables in the past and gave up because it was too much work), check out this list of things you can *stop* doing when you grow vegetables the organic way.

1. STOP **Using Chemicals!**

All good gardens start with healthy soil, and your soil will start getting healthier as soon as you stop using pesticides, herbicides, and synthetic fertilizers. If you put chemicals on your garden, they leach into the soil, which can harm the beneficial insects and micro-organisms that live there. Switching to organic also means you won't be killing off good bugs, so there will be lots more of them around to pollinate vegetables and eat pest insects.

2. STOP **Throwing Kitchen Scraps in the Garbage!**

When you toss out scraps such as eggshells, banana peels, coffee grounds, and apple cores, you're throwing away potential nutrients for your garden. Instead, start a compost pile, add your kitchen scraps to it, and watch them turn into a rich organic amendment for your garden's soil.

Recycle your kitchen scraps in a compost pile, and they'll turn into a rich amendment for your vegetable garden.

3. STOP **Killing Every Caterpillar You Find!**

Yes, some caterpillars are bad bugs and can damage your veggies. But others are good guys and may actually help your garden. So the next time you see a caterpillar hanging out in your vegetable bed, take some time to find out what it is before you squash it. (For a pest identification guide, see "Recommended Reading & Resources" on page 100.)

4. STOP **Compacting Your Soil!**

Every time you step on your garden beds, you're compacting the soil. And the more you compact soil, the more you'll crush the tiny spaces between soil particles where water, air, living creatures, and plant roots should be. Plants need that pore space so their roots can easily penetrate the soil; having that space also allows water to drain through the soil and makes air and nutrients more readily available to plant roots. You can avoid compacting your soil by creating pathways between your beds and by keeping your beds narrow enough to be accessible from the pathways.

5. STOP **Tilling Your Soil to Death!**

You may have been taught to till your garden frequently to control weeds and keep the soil loose and soft. While cultivating the soil can be important, particularly when breaking new ground or adding amendments, too much cultivating can ruin your soil. Tilling repeatedly can cause a rapid loss of organic matter, destroy soil structure, and reduce earthworm populations. A single tilling in the spring, and perhaps another in the fall to turn under crop residues, should be sufficient. In between, work your soil gently with hand tools.

6. STOP **Using Sprinklers!**

Traditional sprinklers deliver water faster than the ground can absorb it, causing the excess to run off,

EXAMINING EARTHWORMS

EARTHWORMS are an indicator of your soil's overall fertility and organic content. The more worms you have, the better! Here's how to check how many earthworms are making their home in your soil.

Pick a day in late spring or early summer when the soil is fairly moist and has warmed to at least 50°F. Dig out a 1-cubic-foot block of your garden soil. Then spread it out. Sift through the soil and count the earthworms (return each one to the hole as you find it and cover it with a bit of soil; worms can't tolerate exposure to the sun). A cubic foot of healthy soil will contain a least ten earthworms.

If your soil is short on earthworms, add lots of compost to it—and stop tilling it so much.

A soaker hose is a better choice than a sprinkler for watering your garden because it gently releases water to plant roots without causing runoff.

which results in soil erosion. The size and speed of the droplets can pummel young seedlings and batter old plants. And sprinklers soak plant foliage, so lots of the water just evaporates instead of reaching the soil and roots. So mulch your garden to conserve moisture, and if you need to water, use a soaker hose to gently and thoroughly wet the soil (for more information on soaker hoses, see "Soaker Hoses" on page 12).

7. STOP Planting the Same Thing in the Same Place Every Year!

Planting the same vegetables in the same place each year can lead to a buildup of soilborne pests and diseases. So to get the most out of your soil and minimize pest and disease problems, you'll need to change where each crop goes from year to year.

8. STOP Avoiding Mulch!

Keeping your vegetable beds covered with a layer of organic mulch is one of the best things you can do

as a gardener. Chopped leaves, straw, grass clippings, or other organic materials control weeds, hold moisture in the soil so you don't have to water as often, help protect plants from some pets, and add organic matter, which in turn improves the soil.

9. STOP Making Poor Planting Decisions!

Do you really need ten zucchini plants? Growing too much of any vegetable is a waste unless you have hungry neighbors with a real fondness for zucchini—or unless you have plenty of time for canning or freezing. Save labor (and your neighbors) by pacing your plantings to match your appetite.

Another poor planting decision is to plant everything at once—resulting in a one-time onslaught of produce. Instead, try planting crops over several weeks throughout the season. The idea is to get as much as you need for a week or two. That way, you'll never be overwhelmed. Planting this way works best with vegetables that ripen all at once, like lettuce, other salad greens, and corn.

10. STOP Making Room for Weeds!

One way to keep weeds from taking over your vegetable garden is to keep your beds full of growing plants. If all the space is occupied, weeds won't have room to sprout.

Again, keeping your soil mulched helps, too, especially if you get caught with nothing growing in your beds. Keep beds mulched with at least 4 inches of shredded leaves, dried grass clippings, or straw.

Also, rake out uninvited sprouts. After digging a new bed, wait a few days for the weeds to sprout (if you can, hang in there until the first rain). Then use a metal rake to scratch the top ½ inch of the soil, which will disrupt any germinating weeds without bringing up lots more.

REDUCING WATER NEEDS

TRY THESE TIPS to reduce water use around your vegetable garden.

- Work organic matter into the soil before planting.

- Space plants just far enough apart so the leaves of mature plants touch; this will shade the soil and reduce evaporation.

- Mulch after planting.

- Make sure rows and beds are level; sloping areas will lose water to runoff.

- Use a ground-level watering system such as a soaker hose; sprinklers lose lots of water to evaporation.

- Don't apply more water than you need to—1 inch a week should do it. If you use a soaker hose, set a household timer to remind you to turn the water off.

Hand tools, such as forks and trowels, are essential to making work in the garden easier and less time-consuming.

Tools & Supplies

You don't need a lot of tools and equipment to grow vegetables, but it's worthwhile to go for the best. A well-constructed tool can make hard work easier and time-consuming tasks shorter. And having the right supplies can help increase yields and reduce pest problems.

GO FOR GOOD QUALITY

Before you buy a tool, try it on for size. Pick it up and go through the motions of using it. The tool should feel comfortable in your hands and shouldn't strain your neck or back. Check the handle height. For tools that you'll use standing up, such as rakes and hoes, the handle should be at least shoulder height. The working end of digging and cultivating tools should be one solid piece of rustproof or rust-resistant metal, such as carbon steel. Heavy digging tools should have what's called solid-socket or solid-strapped construction, which places less stress on the tool head. Be wary of tools that have a blade attached to the handle solely by a metal pin: These tools won't stand up to heavy use.

Take a good look at the handles of the tools you want to buy. Wood handles are strong and durable and feel good in your hands. Fiberglass handles are light and are stronger than wood. Over time, wooden handles wear slightly to become smoother where you put your hands.

HAND TOOLS

You'll want hand tools at the ready every time you visit your vegetable garden. It helps to keep your tools in some type of caddy. You can improvise one from an old bucket, or you can buy one made of fabric or plastic.

7 Essential Vegetable Gardening Tools

- **Garden spade**
- **Digging fork**
- **Garden rake**
- **Row covers**
- **Plant supports**
- **Trowel**
- **Hoe**

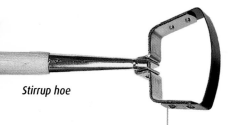

Stirrup hoe

Hoes

You can use hoes to lay out rows, dig furrows, cultivate around plants to loosen the soil and kill weeds, create hills and raised beds, and break up clods. The classic American hoe, with a round-shouldered blade, works well for cultivating around plants and creating furrows for sowing seeds. This hoe comes in a variety of sizes; the bigger the blade, the heavier the work it is intended to do.

There are also many hoes with special blade shapes and designs. Look for a Dutch scuffle hoe or an oscillating stirrup hoe—they're both superb for weeding and light cultivating.

Shovel

Shovels

Shovels are useful for prying out rocks and clumps of roots when you're working the soil for a new garden area. They're also good for digging rounded planting holes, especially if you don't have a garden fork or spade handy. A shovel's head should have a turned edge or footrest to protect your foot when stepping on the shovel to push it into the soil.

Spade

Spades

Spades have a flat, rather than a scooped, blade with squared edges. Use your spade for digging planting holes and digging new garden beds.

Fork

Forks

A spading fork's specialty is cutting into the soil with its four flat or slightly rounded tines. They're the tool of choice for loosening soil in beds before spring planting, mixing materials into the soil, and harvesting potatoes, carrots, and other root crops. Use a pitchfork (three long, rounded tines) or a straw fork (five or six long, rounded tines) for picking up, turning, and scattering hay mulch and light compost material.

Trowels

Use these mini-shovels to dig planting holes for small plants and bulbs, for transplanting seedlings, or for weeding beds and borders. A well-designed trowel won't bend or break when you exert pressure on it.

Trowel

FLOATING ROW COVERS

Floating row covers are among a gardener's best friends when it comes to supplies. One of the greatest uses for row covers, which are made out of spun-bonded synthetic fabric, is pest control. They let air, water, and light pass through, but keep insects *out*. (Row covers do block out about 20 percent of the sun's rays, though.)

You'll want to cover seeds or transplants with floating row covers immediately after planting, so there's no time for pests to find the plants first (otherwise, you'll be trapping the pests inside the cover with your plants).

Anchor the fabric to the ground with metal pins or stones, and spread soil over the edges. Leave enough slack so plants have room to grow. Keep in mind that

quick tip

Don't buy tools with painted handles—the paint may conceal weak wood.

Help protect your plants from pests with floating row covers. They let in light, water, and air but keep insect pests out. If you don't have floating row covers, you can use lightweight plastic.

quick tip

At the end of the gardening season, hose floating row covers off and hang them on a clothesline or spread them out on the lawn to dry. Then roll them up and store them until next season.

some crops, such as squash, need to be pollinated by insects. You'll have to uncover these crops when they bloom or you won't get any fruit. You can leave crops such as carrots and onions covered all season.

Row covers also provide frost protection in spring and fall, act as windbreaks, and even keep your plants cool in summer.

STURDY SUPPORTS

Plant supports fall into one of three categories: stakes, cages, or trellises. Many vegetable plants—notably tomatoes—need help to stand tall under a heavy harvest. While some vegetable crops will produce fruit just fine when sprawled along the ground, they require a lot of space to do so. Plants that touch the ground are also more susceptible to insect pests and soilborne diseases. They're also susceptible to gardener's foot—the flattening experience of being stepped on.

Stakes. Some vegetables, such as peppers and eggplant, may need staking to stand up under their load of fruit. Choose sturdy bamboo or wood that hasn't been treated with chemical preservatives. Insert stakes when plants are very young to avoid injuring their roots. Loosely tie plants to stakes with soft twine or strips of cloth every 8 to 12 inches.

Cages. If you loop a few stakes together with string, you'll form a cage. Or you can roll a length of wire fencing into a tube—the best-known example of this is the tomato cage. Put up your cages when the plants are very small. Cages give plants more room to grow than stakes do, and you don't have to tie the plants to the cages. You should anchor wire cages in place with a stake or metal pins so they won't topple over in a heavy wind.

Trellises. Cucumbers, beans, and other vining crops grow well on trellises. Cucumbers and peas prefer a mesh or netting trellis so their tendrils can curl tightly around the support. Twining vines such as beans spiral around supports as they grow. When building a trellis, use biodegradable string or netting—then just cut the string off at the end of the season and throw it in your compost pile.

Wire cages around plants like tomatoes are great space-savers. They also provide support and protect the fruit from being stepped on.

SOAKER HOSES

Soaker hoses are a simple and inexpensive way to irrigate your garden, and they come in handy when Mother Nature doesn't supply enough rain. Soaker hoses also save water and keep plant leaves dry, which helps eliminate disease problems. Another advantage of soaker hoses is that systems using these hoses need no assembly, and they're easy to lay out between small plants and between narrow row crops like carrots. (Soaker hoses don't work well over long distances, though; they're best for short runs, up to 100 feet, over flat surfaces.)

Some soaker hoses ooze water over their entire length, while others spurt water through tiny holes. If you use a soaker hose with holes, be sure to face the holes downward so the water doesn't squirt up in the air like a sprinkler. Soaker hoses are made of canvas, various plastics, or rubber. Hoses made of rigid plastics or rubber can be hard to lay flat. Plastic and rubber hoses, however, are resistant to fungal attack and

You can lay out a soaker hose right after you've put your transplants in the ground and leave it in place all season, which will make watering less of a chore.

seldom develop leaks at couplings or seams, so you can leave them in the garden for long periods of time and they won't deteriorate. By contrast, canvas hoses are susceptible to mold and mildew, so you should drain and dry them after each use.

COMPOST

Compost is the end result of heaping together waste materials, such as grass clippings and kitchen scraps, and letting them decompose. What you end up with is a nice, rich, organic amendment to add to your soil. Adding compost to your soil makes your garden easier to cultivate, helps to balance the pH, improves moisture retention and root penetration, and converts soil nutrients into a form more easily taken up by plants. You can also use compost as a mulch. Compost isn't difficult to make, and you can make it year-round so that you'll always have a supply on hand. For more on making compost and how to apply it to your soil, see "Making Compost" on page 39.

Animal manures are good sources of organic matter and nutrients, such as nitrogen and potassium. You can use manure as fertilizer by adding it to your compost pile. Don't put raw manure in or on garden soil, though, as it can burn plant roots.

Rock phosphate is one type of organic fertilizer that can give your vegetables a boost. It provides phosphorus, which is critical to plants for growing strong root systems and for overall health and vigor.

Bonemeal is another organic fertilizer that provides phosphorus. However, it's more expensive than rock phosphate.

ORGANIC FERTILIZERS

Finished compost is absolutely the best soil amendment. If you're feeding your soil regularly with compost and keeping it covered with organic mulch, most of your plants won't need any supplemental feedings. However, fertilizers can give crops a boost when:

● You're starting a garden in soil that hasn't been adequately prepared. This can happen when you move to a new home or when you expand your existing garden.

● You're growing crops that benefit from extra fertilizer. Heavy feeders like broccoli and tomatoes love a feeding at planting or a booster feeding to help them along later in the season.

● Your crops' conditions make you suspect that the soil is in worse shape than you thought. If your crops are growing slowly or looking pale, booster feedings may help get them through the season.

If you're making the switch from chemical to organic fertilizers, you may be afraid that using organic fertilizers will be more complicated and less convenient than using premixed chemical fertilizers. Not so! Commercially formulated organic fertilizer blends can be just as

quick tip

If you're digging a new garden or aren't sure what nutrients your soil needs, the best way to find out is to have your soil tested (you can get a test kit from your local extension office). The report you'll receive after you send in your soil sample will tell you whether your soil is acidic or alkaline (soil pH) and how much of the major plant nutrients your soil contains—and it will tell you what to do to adjust these amounts as needed.

convenient and effective as blended synthetic fertilizers. Organic fertilizers differ from chemical ones in that they tend to release nutrients more slowly and in lower concentrations than chemical fertilizers. Unlike their chemical counterparts, many organic fertilizers add organic matter to the soil, as well. Your goal in adding fertilizer is to supply the soil with the three major plant nutrients: nitrogen (N), phosphorus (P), and potassium (K). For specifics on the kinds of organic fertilizers available, see "Fertilizing" on page 42.

TALKING ABOUT TILLERS

TILLERS CAN MAKE quick work of breaking new ground, creating raised beds, and mixing in soil amendments. Power tillers range in size from tiny, 1½ horsepower (HP) models that you can use to work the soil shallowly between rows of crops to full-fledged, 12 HP walk-behind tractors. Most models under 4 HP have front-mounted tines; heavier-duty tillers have rear tines and powered front wheels. When shopping for a tiller, check whether the tilling width can be adjusted, and ask about the length and conditions of the manufacturer's warranty. Whenever practical, though, choose hand tools over tillers. Tillers are expensive and contribute to both air and noise pollution problems. Overusing tillers can also damage the soil and discourage earthworms. If you do use a tiller, avoid tilling deeply, working the soil when it's wet, or pulverizing the top layers of soil too finely.

A bountiful vegetable garden bursting with corn starts with something basic: healthy soil.

Starting a Great Garden

A great vegetable garden starts with great soil. That's because healthy soil will hold more water and feed your plants naturally, so they'll grow vigorously. They'll also be more resistant to attack by insects and infection by disease.

Your payoff for healthy soil (besides lush plants that will produce lots of veggies) will be less time spent watering, fertilizing, and fighting pests. In this chapter, you'll learn how to work and improve your soil to prepare it for planting vegetable seeds and transplants. Before you can get started on soil improvement, though, you'll need to pick a site for your garden.

GETTING STARTED

The key point to remember when planning a vegetable garden, particularly if it's your first one, is to go easy on yourself. Here are some hints for keeping things simple.

Start small. A lot of garden is a lot of work, while a small garden gives you time to tend your crops and figure out what you're doing. Even a space that's 5 × 10 feet can be big enough for a first garden.

Grow vegetables you like. What's the point of growing spinach if nobody in your family—including you—likes it? Ask your family to name their very favorite vegetables, and stick to planting those.

Start with easy crops. Some vegetables are easier to grow than others. Good crops for beginners include green beans, cucumbers, and leaf lettuce.

> **Your payoff for healthy soil will be less time spent watering, fertilizing, and fighting pests.**

Check out your landscape for sun exposure and shade when deciding where to put your garden. Vegetables will produce their best if your garden is in a spot that gets about eight hours of full sun each day.

Choosing the Right Site

Once you've decided what you want to grow, you need to decide where to grow it.

Look on the sunny side. Most veggies need a minimum of five hours of full sun each day, and almost all vegetable crops will produce much better if they receive eight hours of full sun each day.

Plan for easy care. Putting your garden near your house or in a place you walk by every day will make it convenient to stop by daily to weed a bit and check on the progress of the harvest.

Keep air flow in mind. Good air circulation helps prevent disease and reduces damage from late-spring or early-fall frosts. Too much wind, however, can make plants dry out fast. A loose hedge or stand of trees can provide a partial windbreak (just be sure it won't shade your site too much).

Avoid the "big muddy." Many vegetables don't like soggy soil, so before you settle on a site for your garden, wait for rain. Then check to see if water is puddling there, and if it is, how long it takes to dry out. If a wet site is your only option, build raised beds (see "Building Raised Beds" on page 20 for instructions) to improve drainage.

Stay away from black walnut trees. If black walnut trees are in or near your yard, allow clearance of at least one and one-half times the trees' height between tree and garden. That's because these trees produce a substance that inhibits the growth of tomatoes and many other vegetables.

Provide a nearby water source. Make sure your garden is within hose range of a reliable water source. Rainfall doesn't usually provide all the water a garden needs during an entire growing season, and hauling water by hand grows old rather quickly.

PREPARING A GARDEN BED

Once you've decided where to put your garden, you're ready to begin clearing and preparing the site and soil. If you've inherited a recently abandoned garden plot, you'll probably only have to pull out the dead crop plants and weeds. If your site is now a lawn, you'll need to cut the turf out using a spade. Slice under the turf with the spade, and lift it in thin slabs. Pile the cut turf, grass side down, a foot or two high. Keep the pile moist, and the next year it will be a great soil amendment to add to your garden.

Now you're ready to start making the bed.

Begin with cultivating. Cultivating your garden soil is important because it can improve aeration and drainage, allow the roots of your crops to spread more freely, and help break up compacted soil.

You can dig or till your garden a couple of days or a couple of months before you intend to plant. Just make sure the soil isn't too wet when you go to work, or you may end up with large, hard-packed clods of earth that will be impossible to plant in. The soil should be just dry enough to crumble easily in your hand and slide off your spade or fork without sticking. If the soil seems very dry and hard, water the area deeply, then wait two or three days before turning it.

NO ROOM?

YOU CAN STILL plant a vegetable garden, even if you have a small yard. The most important point to remember is to find the sunniest spot you can. Then plant vegetables, such as cucumbers, squash, peas, and beans, that you can train onto trellises. If possible, prepare raised beds with extra-rich soil for your garden (see "Building Raised Beds" on page 20), so you can pack more plants into a small space. Or, be creative and plant a few vegetables in a sunny spot along your driveway or in your flowerbeds. Growing vegetables in containers on your deck or roof is an option, too. Good choices to grow in pots or planters include salad greens such as leaf lettuce, hot pepper plants, and dwarf (compact) tomato varieties.

When preparing a new site for a vegetable bed, add compost to boost the soil's fertility. Spread a 1-inch layer over the top of the bed with a rake, then use a shovel to dig it in.

If you're just starting out in a new garden site, hand tilling offers a big advantage over using a rotary tiller to work the soil. Digging by hand allows you to carefully remove roots, runners, or other parts of perennial weeds as you work. (Using a tiller can make the problem worse by breaking weed roots up into small pieces, and each little piece may then resprout and make a new weed!)

Spread a 1-inch layer of compost over the surface of the soil, then use a shovel or digging fork to dig by hand. A digging fork is best if you're removing weed roots and runners because it's less likely to break them up. A fork is also the best tool for digging rocky soil.

As you dig, work from one end of the bed to the other, turning over the soil to the depth of your shovel or fork. Break up large clods, and remove rocks and weed roots as you go.

Don't stand on the freshly turned soil as you work, and don't walk on it after you've finished. Walking on the soil will destroy the loose, fluffy texture you've worked so hard to create.

BUILDING RAISED BEDS

Although your vegetable crops will thrive in ground-level beds in a well-managed organic soil, they may do even better if you grow them in raised beds. In general, raised beds have better aeration and drainage than ground-level beds because the soil is deeper, looser, and more fertile.

quick tip

Digging a bed doesn't have to be backbreaking work, as long as you keep your knees slightly bent and hold the shovel close to your body when you have lots of soil piled on it.

Making a Mounded Bed

The quickest way to make a raised bed is by mounding. After removing weeds or sod from your chosen site, work the soil with a fork to loosen it, then heap compost and well-rotted manure on top, and rake it together to create a mounded bed. (Try to keep the width of the bed to between 4 and 5 feet, so that you can comfortably reach the middle of the bed without having to stand or walk on it.)

Frame It

You can frame raised beds to keep the soil from eroding and to create nicer-looking beds. Wood, rocks, bricks, or cinder blocks are all good materials for framing raised beds. If you build frames from wood, use naturally rot-resistant woods such as cypress or cedar. Or, if these are too expensive, try oak, which should last for up to ten years without rotting. Avoid commercially pressure-treated wood because it contains toxic materials that may leach into the soil.

You may get even more bounty from your vegetables if you grow them in raised beds. That's because raised beds offer better drainage and aeration than ground-level beds.

ENRICHING THE SOIL

SOIL AMENDMENTS are nutrients you can add to your soil to help improve its health. Organic soil amendments can be made of natural plant or animal materials or of powdered minerals or rock.

Applying soil amendments is a final step after digging a bed. Choose a calm day to do this, because many amendments are powdery. Spread the amendments one at a time on the soil surface. Cover the soil as evenly as possible.

The application instructions on the packaging of your amendment will often tell you how many square feet the package will cover. If you're not sure how thickly to spread the amendment, spread it lightly over the entire area at first. Then go back a second time to use up any remaining amendment. If you're using several amendments, spread a light-colored powder first, then a dark-colored one, then a light. When you're done, till or fork the amendments into the upper 3 to 4 inches of soil.

Thompson & Morgan

TOMATO
Sungold Red F1 Hybrid

893 VEGETABLE

If you start your own transplants from seed, you'll have a lot more varieties to choose from than you would if you bought prestarted seedlings.

Getting Started with Plants & Seeds

The arrival of spring signals the beginning of the gardening season, meaning you don't have to wait any longer to put the ideas you've been thinking about over winter to work. Now's the time to plant seeds or transplants and dream about the fresh, organically grown vegetables you'll be harvesting in the months to come.

Choosing what you're going to grow is one of the best parts about gardening. Love cucumbers, tomatoes, and carrots? Then they're in. Not so keen on beets or zucchini? Then keep them out. Planting a garden is like creating a living masterpiece—and you're the maestro.

The first step toward creating your dream garden is to begin with healthy transplants or seeds. In this chapter, you'll learn what to look for when buying young plants or seeds, along with what you need to know about getting them off to a good start in your garden beds.

> **The first step toward creating your dream garden is to begin with healthy transplants or seeds.**

BUYING PLANTS AND SEEDS

You can kick off your vegetable garden either by planting transplants you've bought at a local garden center (or transplants you've grown yourself; see "Starting Seeds Indoors" on page 29) or by planting seeds directly in the ground. Transplants will give your garden an instant start. Seeds are cheaper than transplants, but they take some time to poke their tiny shoots above ground. No matter which route you choose, keep these points in mind before buying so you get the best possible selection.

Helpful Hints

- **Size up the nursery or garden center.** Are the plants and flats crowded together? Is there adequate airflow to prevent disease?

- **Look at plants carefully.** Seedlings should have short, thick, sturdy stems and deep green foliage. Avoid plants with leaves that are yellow, curled, mottled, or misshapen. Also be wary of big transplants in very tiny containers (they may not have strong root systems).

- **Check the undersides of plant leaves.** You may find insect eggs and pest insects such as aphids, whiteflies, and spider mites.

- **Check the roots.** Take the plant out of its container (ask the nursery for help if you need it) and look at the roots. The soil mass should retain its shape once it's out of the container. Also look for white tips at the roots—they're an indication that the roots are healthy and growing.

- **Check the dates on seed packets.** Old, stale seed doesn't germinate reliably, so if the seed isn't marked for the current growing season, don't buy it—or be prepared for spotty germination.

Before buying a transplant, carefully take the plant out of its container to check the roots. Look for white tips at the roots' ends, which means the roots are healthy.

HOW TO READ A SEED PACKET

THE BACK OF A SEED packet contains valuable growing information about the plant. Here's how to decipher it. (Keep in mind that packets of organically grown seed—that is, seeds produced in accordance with the standards of an organic certification organization—will be labeled as such on the packet.)

Number of Plants

Some packets have specific seed counts to help you figure out how many packets to buy. Other packets, like this one, list the approximate number of plants you should be able to grow from the amount of seed in the packet, without listing a specific seed count.

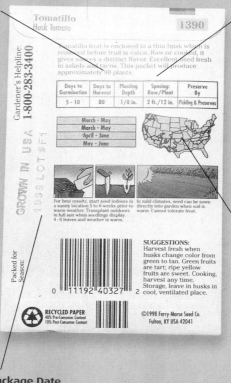

Planting Information

You can find advice on how deep to plant the seed, how long it will take to sprout, and how long it will be until you can harvest the vegetables.

Planting Map

Figure out where you are on the map, then refer to the color guide to determine the prime time for planting outdoors in your area.

Package Date

This date indicates that the seed met or exceeded the federal standards for minimum germination when tested for that year.

DON'T THROW AWAY those half-full seed packets. Many crop seeds will stay viable for several years if you store them in a cool, dry place. The life expectancy of vegetable seeds ranges from only one year up to six years.

Beans: 3 years

Beets: 4 years

Broccoli: 3 years

Cabbages: 4 years

Carrots: 3 years

Cauliflower: 4 years

Corn: 2 years

Cucumbers: 5 years

Eggplant: 4 years

Lettuces: 6 years

Onions: 1 year

Peas: 3 years

Peppers: 2 years

Radishes: 5 years

Spinach: 3 years

Squash: 4 years

Deciding When to Plant

Knowing what conditions your veggies need will help you pick the best time to begin planting. Seed packets and seedling labels usually give general guidelines on the best planting times, but here are some basic pointers.

Cool-season crops. Peas, lettuce, carrots, beets, and several other crops are ready for planting as soon as the soil has thawed and dried out enough for you to work it in the spring.

Warm-season crops. Beans and squash won't grow well until the soil has warmed, so wait to plant them around the last spring frost date. (If you don't know your last frost date, contact your local extension office or ask a knowledgeable neighbor.)

Cold-sensitive crops. Corn and tomatoes won't be ready to go in the ground until about two weeks after your last frost date.

Seeds or Plants?

You may be wondering how to decide when to buy seeds and when to buy transplants. One thing to keep in mind is that buying seeds offers a few advantages that buying transplants doesn't. If you start from seed, you can grow crops and varieties, such as brussels sprouts and heirloom tomatoes, that aren't widely available as prestarted seedlings. In fact, you'll have many more varieties of each vegetable to choose from if you go the seed-starting route.

Also, for crops like beans and peas, planting seeds directly in the garden is the best method because the seedlings won't adapt well to being transplanted.

Plant as Seed

- Beans
- Beets
- Carrots
- Cucumbers
- Peas
- Potatoes
- Salad greens
- Squash
- Sweet corn

Plant as Transplants

- Broccoli
- Cabbage
- Peppers
- Tomatoes

Onions and Garlic

Onions and garlic are different than other veggies. To grow them, you plant sets, or immature bulbs, instead of seeds or seedlings. Plant them as you would transplants (see below).

Planting Transplants

You can move transplants from containers into their new home in your garden in seven easy steps. For best results, move transplants to the garden on a cool, still, overcast day, or later in the afternoon. Otherwise, sun and wind can dry out the seedlings, hindering their growth or even killing them.

1. Using a trowel, dig a hole fairly deep and about 1½ times as wide as the container that's holding the transplant. (You want to be able to set the transplants lower than they grew in the pots.)

2. Take the transplant out of its container. If the container is flexible plastic, you should be able to gently squeeze the sides to loosen the soil and roots; if the container isn't flexible, turn the plant upside down and tap firmly on the container's bottom.

After planting a transplant outdoors, make sure to firmly pat the soil around the hole. Watering is also essential to help get your new transplant off to a good start after it's in place in your garden.

HILL PLANTING CONSISTS of small groups of seeds with wide spaces between the groups. It doesn't necessarily imply an actual mound, although planting on low mounds can improve drainage and reduce the chance of seed decay. Vining crops, such as melons, squash, and pumpkins, are common choices for hill planting.

Use rocks or stakes to lay out the spacing of your hills. Plant two or three seeds in each spot at the correct depth, and cover as needed.

Once the seeds are covered, pat the planted area with your fingers or the back of a rake to get good contact between the seed and the soil. Label the hill, and water gently to moisten the soil.

3. Turn the plant right side up and put the root-ball into the hole you've prepared. (Try to keep as much soil on the rootball as possible.)

4. Fill the hole around the rootball with the soil you removed when you dug the hole, then pat the hole firmly. (Keep the soil level around the stem.)

5. Water each transplant as soon as you plant it; when you're done planting for the day, water everything thoroughly.

6. If you had to plant on a sunny day or if the weather is supposed to be sunny and hot for the next few days, give the transplants a little shade (propped-up pieces of cardboard will do the trick).

7. If the weather is still a little cool, protect the transplants by putting paper bags over them at night. Cut partway up the sides of the bags and weight down the flaps with either soil or small rocks.

PLANTING CROPS FROM SEED

Planting seeds directly in your garden is really just as easy as putting transplants in the ground. Here's how to do it.

1. Use your finger or a trowel to prepare a shallow trench (see the seed packet for how deep and far apart to plant the seeds).

2. To plant small seeds, pour some seeds from the packet into the palm of one hand. Using your other hand, pick up a few seeds between your fingers and scatter them down the trench. (Don't worry about sowing seeds too close together; you can always pull extra seedlings out once they come up.)

3. To plant larger vegetable seeds, use your finger to poke holes in the soil the correct depth and distance apart. Pick out individual seeds and carefully drop one in each hole.

4. Once you've planted the seeds, sprinkle soil over the row, then lightly pat down the soil.

5. Give your newly seeded rows a gentle but thorough watering.

Don't worry about sowing seeds too close together when you plant them directly in the ground. You can always pull out some seedlings once they sprout to set the proper spacing.

STARTING SEEDS INDOORS

Starting seeds indoors is a little trickier than planting directly outdoors, but it gives you a head start on the gardening season because you can get crops started indoors while it's still too cold to plant them outside.

For crops like tomatoes and peppers, starting seeds indoors is the only do-it-yourself option. In most areas, if you planted these seeds directly outdoors, the crops wouldn't have enough time to grow and bear fruit before cool weather and frost arrive, ending the season.

The Basics

Here are some helpful tips to ensure your success with starting seeds indoors.

Start with a light soil mix. Seeds contain their own food supply, so they don't need rich soil right away. What they do need to grow into strong

GIVING SEEDLINGS MORE ROOM

THE FIRST LEAVES that your seedlings produce are called the seed leaves. The second set of leaves are called the first true leaves. When the first true leaves open up, it's time to transplant your seedlings to pots or to wider spacing (about 2 inches apart) in a larger flat. Water your seedlings the day before you plan to transplant them so the seed-starting mix will be moist and cling to the roots. Fill the new containers about two-thirds full with potting soil and poke holes in the soil for the seedlings. Then carefully prick out one plant at a time using a pencil. Select the sturdiest, strongest seedlings, and discard the rest. Settle the seedlings in the new potting soil and fill in more potting soil around them until you have at least matched the depth of the old soil. Water the plants from the bottom up and keep them out of direct light for a day to let the roots recover, then return them to a bright window or a fluorescent light setup.

seedlings is moisture, air, and a loose planting medium (the stuff your seeds will sprout in) so their tender new roots can easily stretch and grow. A commercial seed-starting mix will do the trick, or you can make your own by mixing equal parts vermiculite, milled sphagnum moss (or screened compost), and perlite—all available at garden supply stores.

Choose a container that drains well. Seed-starting containers should have drainage holes in the bottom so seedling roots don't get waterlogged. Recycled cell packs (like the kind you buy prestarted plants in) and cut-down plastic jugs or milk cartons all work well, as long as they have drainage holes in them. If you recycle cell packs, be sure to wash them thoroughly with soap and hot water to kill disease-causing organisms before reusing the packs for seed starting.

Prewet the mix. It's important to plant seeds in moist mix because if you try to water newly planted seeds (especially very tiny ones), you'll probably wash them all to one corner of the container or bury them too deeply. To moisten dry mix, put it in a bucket, add some warm water, and stir. Keep adding water until the mix is evenly moist—only a few drops of water should ooze out when you squeeze a handful of it. If the mix is too wet, try adding more dry mix.

Sow thinly. Seedlings that are crowded will have stems that are long, weak, and pale from their search for light and space.

Know your depth. You don't want to bury the seeds too deep, or they may not germinate. A general rule of thumb is to cover the seed with an amount of soil equal to three times the thickness of the seed.

The Next Steps

Keep them warm and wet. Warmth and moisture are what switch a seed's slumbering metabolism into high gear. Most vegetable seeds germinate best at a comfortably warm temperature, roughly 70°F—which is probably warmer than your house. That means you'll need to find a warm spot for your seedling containers. You can put them on top of your refrigerator or your water heater or on a shelf above a radiator. The area doesn't have to be well lit; you can move the container to a brighter spot when the seeds sprout. If you don't have a warm spot, you can buy a small heating coil or mat specifically designed for seed starting.

You also need to keep your seeds damp—but not wet. The best way to do that is to water from below. Either set the flat in a larger basin of water and allow it to absorb moisture for several hours, or pour water into a tray in which your planted cell packs or individual pots are sitting.

quick tip

Some seedlings, such as cucumbers and squash, don't like their roots disturbed. If you need to thin these seedlings out, use sharp scissors to cut off unwanted seedlings at soil level instead of transplanting the seedlings you're keeping.

One key to growing transplants like these pea seedlings successfully is to keep them moist by watering from below.

quick tip

Prevent your seedlings from falling over (otherwise known as damping-off) by sterilizing recycled containers before planting. Dip old plastic flats and pots in a 10 percent bleach solution (1 cup bleach to 9 cups of water). Rinse, then air-dry.

If you end up with leggy seedlings that flop over, the plants are either not getting enough light or are too crowded.

Give 'em light. Once your seedlings break the surface of the mix, they need plenty of light. A large window, preferably a south-facing one, provides enough light for most seedlings. Turn the container daily to keep the stems from developing a permanent bend toward the light. If window space is limited, set your seedlings under lights (you can use those two-bulb fluorescent shop-light fixtures). Place the seedlings about 2 to 4 inches from the tubes, and give them 14 to 16 hours of light a day.

Transplant Troubleshooting

What if no seedlings appear, or the ones that do seem fine at first and then begin to die? Use the following information to help you troubleshoot if a problem threatens your tiny charges.

Low or no germination. If your containers fail to fill with seedlings after ample time has passed, one or more of these things may have happened: Tem-

peratures were too low or too high, planting depth wasn't correct, seeds were old, or you let the soil dry out. Resow the seeds or change the conditions and wait a little longer.

Leggy seedlings. Tall, leggy stems mean seedlings are struggling to get enough light, are too crowded, or are kept too warm. Supplement windowsill lighting with fluorescent shop lights, or thin crowded seedlings. If you think they're too warm, move them to a cooler place. Plant leggy seedlings deeper than usual when transplanting them outdoors.

Discolored leaves. If your seedlings outgrow the nutrients stored in their seeds and seed leaves, their foliage may turn colors, depending on the nutrients they lack. (Yellow leaves, for example, are usually a sign of nitrogen deficiency, while bronze leaves indicate a need for potassium.) Water with fish emulsion (a type of commercial organic fertilizer) once true leaves develop. You can also water with compost tea (see "Liquid Fertilizers" on page 43 for how to make it).

Shriveled seedlings. Seedlings that look fine one day but are keeled over the next are victims of damping-off. If the stems have shriveled and collapsed at the point where they touch the soil, the culprit is probably the kind of soilborne fungi that thrive in damp, poorly ventilated spaces. To spare yourself damping-off disappointment in the future, keep your planting flats clean and use fresh seed-starting mix for each batch of seeds. Avoid overwatering and be sure your containers are well drained. Thin seedlings so that air can circulate between them. And keep your soil level high so that the sides of the container don't block air currents.

GETTING TOUGH

YOU HAVE TO TOUGHEN UP your transplants before you move them outdoors or they'll be shocked by the stronger wind, cooler air, and brighter light. This toughening up is known as hardening off.

You should begin hardening off your seedlings one to two weeks before you transplant. Set them outside, preferably in a spot where they'll receive direct sun in the morning and bright, but indirect, light in the afternoon. You can do this in stages, leaving the plants outside for an increasing number of hours each day and bringing them in each night. After about a week, start leaving the seedlings outdoors overnight; protect frost-tender crops such as tomatoes by hardening them off on the porch or in a cold-frame. Once they become accustomed to the outside world, they're ready to move into their permanent homes in your garden.

Keys to keeping your garden in top shape include watering, mulching, and weeding.

Managing Your Garden

Once your vegetable seeds and transplants are in the ground, the fun begins! Beans will sprout, tomato plants will start to fill their cages, and cucumber vines will ramble across their beds. Your job now is to keep your plants growing strong.

Managing a vegetable garden means supplying enough water when Mother Nature doesn't, getting rid of weeds, adding mulch, and feeding your plants with fertilizer or compost. Providing all of these things will go a long way toward producing a bountiful organic harvest.

As the harvest dwindles and summer changes to fall, you'll spend time getting your garden ready for winter. Post-harvest cleanup is well worth the effort because when spring rolls around the following year, you'll be able to plant as soon as the soil is warm enough to work.

Weeding and mulching go a long way toward producing a bountiful organic harvest.

WATERING

Vegetables grow best in soil that's constantly moist; if the top 1 or 2 inches of soil dries out, plants become stressed. That's why your plants will be happiest if you water them before the soil gets dry. A general rule of thumb to follow is to supply 1 inch of water per week. (Of course, you'll have to modify that depending on weather conditions.)

When to Water

Early morning is an ideal time to water because water soaks in before heat causes it to evaporate. Plus, the day's warmth dries your plants' leaves before nightfall, reducing the spread of disease. If you don't

have time to water in the morning, don't worry—evening watering is a good option, too, as long as you can avoid getting water on the leaves.

Ways to Water

Watering can or hose. Hand-watering your plants with a watering can or hose is the least complicated method. If you do hand-water, use a water breaker or "rose" to divide the water flow into a gentle sprinkle that will soak into the ground and not disturb your plants. Stand close to the plant you're watering so you can direct the water at the soil under the plant rather than at the leaves.

Soaker hoses. Soaker hoses are water-efficient, in-expensive, and easy to use. They also keep leaves dry, which helps to avoid disease problems. Some soaker hoses ooze water over their entire length; others spurt water through tiny holes. If you use a soaker hose

SAVING RAIN

YOU CAN HELP conserve water by saving rain for watering your vegetable plants. Just place a barrel under one of the downspouts on your house so the rainwater can run right into the barrel. (You might need to set the barrel on a couple of cinder blocks so the mouth of the downspout is relatively close to the opening of the barrel.) A spigot near the bottom of the barrel makes it easy to fill your watering can. You can buy a ready-made rain barrel complete with spigot, or improvise your own from a heavy-duty plastic trash can.

with holes, be sure to face the holes downward so the water doesn't squirt up in the air like a sprinkler. (See "Soaker Hoses" on page 12 for more information.)

Sprinklers. Traditional oscillating sprinklers and rotating impact sprinklers can cover lots of garden with lots of big drops of water. In fact, they deliver water faster than the ground can absorb it, causing the excess to run off the surface. And the size and speed of the drops can pummel young seedlings and batter old plants. So don't use your sprinkler to water your vegetable garden. You'll get much better results watering by hand or using a soaker hose.

Sprinklers can work well for keeping new seedbeds moist. Choose a sprinkler that breaks up the water into fine drops, and set it to sprinkle only the area you want to water. To prevent runoff, put the sprinkler on a timer to run only 10 to 20 minutes an hour, two or three times a day. That way the water will have time to soak into the soil between waterings.

MULCHING

Putting mulch on your garden is one of the best things you can do for your plants. A thick layer of organic mulch over the soil blocks weeds, keeps the soil cool and moist, provides a home for good bugs such as spiders and ground beetles, and, as the mulch decays, feeds both the soil and the plants growing in it. Plus, it's easy to find lots of organic mulch materials around your yard.

Grass clippings. If your lawn can't supply enough grass clippings for your garden, check with a local lawn-care service or a neighbor for extra clippings. Don't use clippings from herbicide-treated lawns or that contain grass plants or weeds that have gone to seed. (If you're not sure, play it safe and don't use them.) Apply a 4-inch layer of loose clippings or a 1- to 2-inch layer of compressed clippings.

quick tip

Wood chips are a good mulch for vegetable garden pathways. Spread the wood chips on bare soil before any weeds come up because wood chips are better at stopping weeds from sprouting than they are at smothering existing weeds.

Have fun with those fall leaves, then shred them up and use them for mulch in your garden.

Shredded leaves. This is the best mulch for attracting earthworms. Use a 4-inch layer of loose leaves or a 1- to 2-inch layer of compressed leaves.

Straw. Straw protects plants such as tomatoes against soil-dwelling diseases by providing a barrier between the fruit and the soil. Spread a 4-inch layer of loose straw.

Compost. Compost helps prevent diseases, and it feeds plants. Spread it 1 to 2 inches thick. (See the opposite page for tips on making compost.)

Newspaper. Spread sheets of newspaper (about 4 sheets thick) or a 6-inch layer of shredded paper. Top newspaper with compost, grass, or straw to keep it from blowing away.

Pine needles. Despite what you may have heard, pine needles won't acidify your soil when used as mulch. Use a 1- to 2-inch layer.

Wait until your plants are well established before mulching because some mulches release substances that are toxic to seedlings. Another point to keep in mind is that the more coarse a mulch is, the less it will improve soil moisture retention. This means coarse mulches, such as straw, may be a good choice for cool, wet, or heavy soils. Sandy, light, or well-drained soils do well with fine-textured mulches, such as partially decomposed sawdust, that hold in moisture.

MAKING COMPOST

Every vegetable gardener should make compost. Composting is easy to do, and the end result is a great mulch and slow-release fertilizer all in one. You can make compost throughout the vegetable gardening season, and you can even set up a compost pile right in or beside your vegetable garden.

Compost Ingredients

Compost is nothing more than grass clippings, kitchen scraps, crop residues, weeds—or almost any other organic matter—that's been piled together long enough to decompose completely. A compost pile needs both carbon-rich materials (called "browns") and nitrogen-rich materials (called "greens") in order for the decomposer organisms to produce compost efficiently. Mixing roughly two to three times as much "brown" material by bulk as "green" is the ratio you want to try to reach so your pile heats up and decomposes.

Building a Pile

You can make compost in a freestanding heap or by piling the materials in a compost bin. (Buy a

A compost pile is pretty low maintenance, although you do need to turn it once in a while. The more you turn it, the faster its contents will decompose.

COMPOST INGREDIENTS

High-Carbon "Browns"
Dry leaves, weeds, cover crops

Chopped cornstalks

Hay

Nutshells

Paper (moderate amounts)

Aged sawdust

Straw

High-Nitrogen "Greens"
Coffee grounds

Fruit scraps

Fresh grass clippings

Fresh leaves (avoid walnut and eucalyptus)

Green manure crops

Manure (cow, fowl, horse, pig, sheep; *not* cat or dog droppings)

Seaweed

Tea bags

Vegetable scraps

Weeds

THE EASIEST WAY to get plenty of air, which is important for decomposition, into a compost pile is to turn the pile from time to time. But if you build your pile in a compost bin, as opposed to a freestanding heap, also make sure that that bin has openings in the sides or the bottom to provide much-needed ventilation.

A PVC pipe with holes drilled through it stuck upright in the center of the pile will aerate it. You can also put poles upright in the pile as you build it and pull them out when you're finished to create airways. Or just poke holes in the pile occasionally with a pry bar or the handle of a hoe or rake.

commercial bin or make your own—both welded wire and cinder blocks work well for making bins.)

To build a pile, either make separate alternating layers of browns and greens, or just dump or shovel on some of each and mix them with a garden fork. Sprinkle the materials with water as you go. The more mixed your pile is, the faster it's likely to become finished compost.

Maintaining a Pile

Once built, all you need to do to your pile is turn it once in a while: Fork the materials from the inside to the outside and from the bottom to the top. The more often you turn the pile, the more air will get into it, and the faster its contents will decompose. And, unless you live in an arid climate, cover the top of the pile with a tarp or a layer of straw to keep rain from waterlogging the pile and from washing nutrients away.

WEEDING

While you don't need to eliminate every single weed from your vegetable garden, it's important to keep weeds under control. That's because weeds steal important nutrients and moisture from the soil at the expense of your vegetables. Weeds can also block air circulation and cast shadows that prevent your vegetable plants from soaking up the sun.

Presprout Your Weeds

Presprouting is an easy and effective technique for getting weeds under control before you plant your vegetable crops.

1. As you prepare the soil in spring, dig out as many weed roots as you can.

2. Add any needed amendments to the soil, rake the area smooth, then water it. Keep the soil moist for seven to ten days, until it's covered with weed seedlings 1 or 2 inches high.

3. Carefully pull out the shoots and roots of as many weeds as you can, then use a scuffle hoe to cut through the remaining weed seedlings just below the soil surface.

Dandelions and other weeds steal important nutrients and moisture from the soil and away from your vegetables. So while you don't need to eliminate every weed from your garden, you do need to keep them under control.

Weeding Wisdom

To avoid having to fight an overwhelming weed invasion, follow these tips for making the most out of your weeding time.

- Control weeds when they're small. A hoe works best on weed seedlings; hand-pull larger weeds.

- Cultivate shallowly to avoid bringing more weed seeds to the surface.

- Always pull weeds before they set seed.

- Weed when the soil is moist, if possible; the weeds will be easier to pull.

- Don't give up on weeding in the winter. A few short weeding sessions on mild days will keep cool-season weeds such as chickweed under control.

FERTILIZING

Fertilizer is icing on the cake for plants growing in rich, organic soil. In fact, if you improve your soil from year to year with lots of compost and other organic material, chances are you'll have a great harvest without having to add fertilizer. Some vegetables though, such as tomatoes, benefit from extra fertilizer. And once in a while you may notice that your crops look pale green or are growing slowly. Those symptoms show that your soil isn't as nutrient-rich as you thought it was—so your crops will need a boost.

Dry Fertilizers

Popular dry fertilizers include bloodmeal, bonemeal, cottonseed meal, and rock phosphate. Apply these materials by side-dressing—working them into the top 1 inch of soil next to, but not touching, the plants.

Bloodmeal. A slaughterhouse by-product, bloodmeal is dried, ground blood. It's a potent nitrogen

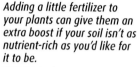
Adding a little fertilizer to your plants can give them an extra boost if your soil isn't as nutrient-rich as you'd like for it to be.

source, so use it sparingly. If your soil is average, add 1 to 2 pounds of bloodmeal per 100 square feet before planting your crops. If nitrogen-hungry crops (such as tomatoes) seem to need a boost during the growing season, side-dress them lightly with bloodmeal. Water the bloodmeal into the soil after you apply it.

Bonemeal. This fertilizer, which provides phosphorus, is also a slaughterhouse by-product; specifically, it's ground animal bones. Apply 2 pounds per 100 square feet on average soils.

Cottonseed meal. Cottonseed meal is the waste left over after pressing cottonseed oil; it provides nitrogen. Keep in mind, though, that cotton is usually sprayed with pesticides, which contaminate the cottonseed meal. Use 2 to 4 pounds per 100 square feet if your soil's organic matter is average.

Rock phosphate. This phosphorus fertilizer is the mined skeletal remains of prehistoric animals. Rock phosphate provides more phosphorous than bonemeal and costs less. Use 2 to 2½ pounds per 100 square feet if your soil's organic matter is average.

Liquid Fertilizers

Liquid fertilizers, such as seaweed extract, fish emulsion, and compost tea, are especially good choices for booster feedings because the nutrients in them are quickly available to plants. You can water liquid fertilizers into the soil or spray them directly on the plant leaves.

Apply seaweed extract and fish emulsion at the rates specified on the package label. To make compost tea, add about 2 cups of compost to a gallon of water and let it steep for three days. Filter the mixture through burlap or cheesecloth, and return the trapped solids to the compost pile or garden. Place the strained liquid in a small sprayer or watering can and use.

FIXING DEFICIENCIES

IF YOUR VEGETABLES suffer from a nutrient deficiency, you probably won't notice the symptoms until it's too late to do anything about them because vegetables grow so fast. What you can do, though, is to fight back by working harder to improve overall soil fertility. Include a soil test in your plans for the following year. The test results will help you plan a program of amendments to revitalize your soil.

Signs of Soil Stress

Beets. Poor growth may indicate a nitrogen deficiency.

Potatoes. Sickly potatoes may signal low potassium levels.

Carrots. Struggling carrots may indicate a potassium and phosphorus deficiency.

Tomatoes. Plants blossom but few or no fruit may signal excessive nitrogen.

Beans. Stunted plants with light green to yellow leaves may signal a nitrogen deficiency.

COMPANION PLANTING

Planting certain plants together in your garden to confuse or repel plant pests or attract beneficial insects (lady beetles and other insects that eat pests) is a technique called companion planting. Companion planting practices combine both folklore and fact—some practices are garden lore that have never been scientifically proven. However, research shows that some companion plants really have a significant beneficial effect for their neighboring crops.

Repel with Smell

Pests sometimes locate plants by "smell." If pests can't smell your plants, or if the scent isn't right, they might go elsewhere. So to mask the smell of vulnerable vegetable crops, disguise them by pairing them with plants that have a repellent or masking fragrance. Here are some good choices:

Marigolds. Plant them as thickly as you can in your vegetable bed (keep in mind that this won't work if you use unscented marigolds).

Mints. Cabbage pests and aphids dislike catnip and some other members of this fragrant family. Because mints can grow out of control, don't plant them directly in your garden. Instead, place potted mints around your garden bed.

quick tip

Nasturtiums planted among vegetables deter whiteflies and squash bugs, but they work even better as a trap crop (a crop planted to attract a specific insect pest) for aphids, which prefer nasturtiums to other plants.

Companion Planting Combos

VEGETABLE	COMBINE WITH	BENEFITS
Tomatoes	Basil	Controls tomato hornworms
Cabbage	Thyme or tomatoes	Controls flea beetles, cabbage maggots, white cabbage butterflies, imported cabbageworms
Carrots	Onions	Controls rust flies
Potatoes	Horseradish	Repels Colorado potato beetles
Cucumbers	Radishes	Controls cucumber beetles

Rue. Oils from the leaves of rue give some people a poison-ivy-like rash, so use this plant with care. However, what annoys people also deters Japanese beetles. Grow rue as a garden border, or scatter clippings near beetle-infested crops.

Sweet basil. Interplant this culinary herb in your vegetable garden to repel aphids, mosquitoes, and mites.

Tansy. Used as a mulch, tansy may cause cucumber beetles, Japanese beetles, ants, and squash bugs to go elsewhere. Take note, though, that tansy does attract pesky imported cabbageworms.

Help protect your tomatoes from tomato hornworms by growing basil between the plants.

Flowers to the Rescue

Another companion planting technique involves interplanting certain flowers (called host plants) with your vegetables to attract specific beneficial insects. The flowers provide shelter and food for the beneficials they attract. (Many beneficial insects eat nectar as well as pest insects.)

Plants that have very small flowers are good choices to plant for beneficial insects. That's because beneficials have short mouthparts and can't reach deep into flowers for food. To help beneficial insects become established in your garden early on, plant gazanias, calendulas, or other small-flowered plants that will bloom even in early-season cool weather. And keep on planting a variety of flowers because beneficials need blossoms to sustain them from spring through fall.

FAMILY MATTERS

RELATED CROPS belong to what are called botanical families. Here's a list of common botanical families and some of their members.

Beet family: beet, chard, spinach

Cabbage family: broccoli, brussels sprouts, cabbage, cauliflower, collard, kale, kohlrabi, radish, turnip

Carrot family: carrot, celery, chervil, cilantro, dill, parsley, parsnip

Grass family: corn

Lettuce family: artichoke, chicory, endive, lettuce

Lily family: chives, garlic, leek, onion

Pea family: bean, cowpea, pea, peanut

Squash family: cucumber, melon, pumpkin, squash

Tomato family: eggplant, pepper, potato, tomato

Here are some examples of flowers and herbs that attract beneficials:

- Angelica
- Candytuft
- Dill
- Evening primrose
- Fennel
- Golden marguerite
- Goldenrod
- Morning glory
- Sweet alyssum
- Yarrow

CROP ROTATION

Some vegetable crops demand a lot from the soil, while others don't. For example, broccoli, corn, and tomatoes are heavy feeders that rapidly use up nitrogen, while root vegetables, such as carrots and beets, are light feeders. So to keep soil nutrients balanced throughout your garden, avoid planting the same vegetables in the same place year after year.

Keep a map or notes about your garden plan every year so you can refer to the previous year's and see where each vegetable grew. Then choose a different area or bed in which to grow each vegetable this year. This technique is known as crop rotation.

Here's a good general rotation to follow:

- **First year:** Fruit crops such as tomatoes, broccoli, corn, and squash
- **Second year:** Root crops such as carrots, potatoes, and onions
- **Third year:** Leafy crops such as lettuce, spinach, and cabbage

Peas and beans can fit into a rotation such as this at any time.

Rotating for Pest and Disease Control

Rotating crops from year to year also helps reduce the buildup of some pests and disease organisms in the soil. However, rotating crops for this purpose is a

little trickier than rotating to balance soil nutrients because some diseases and pests can attack several types of crops, not just one. For example, late blight affects both potatoes and tomatoes. To be successful, you need to avoid replanting any of a particular vegetable's relatives in the bed where that vegetable grew last year. For example, tomatoes, peppers, and eggplants are related crops, so you shouldn't plant tomatoes where peppers or eggplants grew last year.

You can also avoid persistent pests, such as cabbage root maggots, by planting your crop before the pest becomes active in the spring. You'll need to learn about the pest's life cycle to determine if timed planting will work (a good insect identification guide can help; see "Recommended Reading & Resources" on page 100). To find out when various pests become active in your region, contact your local extension office.

Changing where you plant vegetables from year to year is important in maintaining balanced soil nutrients. Keep notes about your garden plan every year so you can refer to your notes when planning the next year's garden.

ENDING THE SEASON

As the fruits of your labors start to dwindle after the first fall frost, you might be tempted to forget your garden until next spring. But it's worth your time now to clean up the debris and protect the plants and soil so that you'll get your garden off to a healthy start next season.

quick tip

Here's a way to recycle old cornstalks after harvest. Just pull them up, tie several together, then stick the whole thing in the middle of your compost pile. The stalks will help air reach the center of the pile.

Garden Cleanup

- Pull or cut weeds before they can form seed.

- Pull out spent vegetable plants after they're finished bearing.

- Collect stakes, temporary trellises, and row covers, and scrape off clinging soil. To remove insect eggs, rinse the materials in a solution of 1 part bleach to 9 parts water. Spread them out to dry in the sun before storing for the winter.

- Pick any remaining vegetables.

Settling Soil for the Winter

You have three options for dealing with your garden soil at the end of the season, depending on the amount of time and the materials you have.

1. **Mulch it.** In cold areas with little snow cover, mulching after the ground has frozen helps moderate soil temperatures, which is good for helpful soil organisms such as earthworms. In areas with mild, wet winters, mulch prevents heavy rains from eroding bare soil.

2. **Cultivate, then mulch it.** Fall digging or tilling has several advantages. It can kill pests that are in the soil or expose them to birds or other predators. Fall digging can also bury plant debris that might harbor overwintering insects. In the spring, tilled soil warms faster, so you can plant

Don't forget about your garden after the first fall frost. In fact, that's the time to clean it up so it's in good shape for the start of the next gardening season.

sooner. On the downside, fall tilling can increase weed seed germination in the spring (although a mulch should help prevent some weeds from sprouting.)

3. **Cultivate, then plant a cover crop.** Growing a cover crop over winter will protect your soil from erosion and enrich it at the same time. Dig or till the soil in late summer or early fall, then sow grains like oats or wheat; or plant legumes, such as fava beans or red clover. Then work the plants into the soil before spring planting to release organic matter and nutrients.

Encouraging helpful insects like lady beetles to visit your garden is an easy but important part of fighting pests the organic way.

Fighting Pests the Organic Way

When you plant vegetables, bugs will come. But don't assume that all beetles, caterpillars, and other creatures that find their way into your garden are bad. Most are actually helpful to gardeners—that's why they're called "beneficials." Beneficial insects eat the nasty guys and help pollinate plants.

It's important to know what the good guys look like, so you don't mistakenly try to vanquish them from your garden. In fact, *encouraging* beneficials is a critical part of controlling pests organically. So is using barriers such as floating row covers to protect your plants from pest damage. Occasionally, a pest problem may flare up, and you'll need to take the bad guys out of action—we'll explain safe, chemical-free ways to do so.

The garden-fresh goodness filling your vegetable beds is a beacon for bigger critters, too, like deer and raccoons. Although these animals look cute, what they can do to your garden won't leave you laughing. Later in this chapter, you'll learn how to beat them at their own game.

> **Encouraging beneficials is a critical part of controlling pests organically.**

7 LOW-TECH WAYS TO CONTROL PESTS

Here are seven easy, inexpensive ways to keep bad bugs from getting the better of your garden.

1. Keep a clean garden. Always pull out any badly infested plants during the growing season and clean up spent plants when they're finished producing. Doing so denies pest insects a place to hide over the winter months.

2. **Get in the hand-picking habit.** Walk through your garden daily with a bucket of soapy water in tow. Pick off offenders and drop them into the bucket.

3. **Control aphids, small caterpillars,** and other nuisances with a strong spray of water from your garden hose.

4. **Ring your seedlings.** Cardboard (use toilet paper cylinders and paper towel tubes cut into smaller sections) or aluminum foil collars will keep pests from chewing tender stems. Push the collar into the soil around the transplant right after planting.

5. **Mix things up.** Confuse pests by intermingling different crops in your beds—mix veggies with herbs and flowers—so that pests can't zero in on one crop (for more on this method, see "Companion Planting" on page 44).

6. **Invite good bugs in.** Plant dill, fennel, coriander, sweet alyssum, and other small-flowered plants that attract beneficial insects (such as lady beetles) to feed on their nectar.

7. **Mulch pests away.** Mulches can help control pests by repelling or confusing them. Colorado potato beetles, for instance, have a harder time zeroing in on potato plants mulched with straw than they do on unmulched potatoes. And reflective mulches (like aluminum foil) have been found to help keep aphids off summer squash.

8 GARDEN GOOD GUYS

It's easy to encourage beneficials to take up residence in your vegetable garden. Many common beneficials need nothing more than an undisturbed area for shelter and some flowering nectar plants to supplement their diet of pest insects. Here are eight of the most common beneficials you may spot hanging around in your vegetable garden.

-- SOLDIER BEETLE -----------------------

Adults (also called leatherwings) resemble fireflies but don't glow, are ½ inch long or smaller, and are usually dark with orange, yellow, or red markings. Soldier beetle larvae are usually dark-colored, flat, long, and segmented, with many fine hairs and a velvety appearance.

Welcome soldier beetles into your garden by planting lots of nectar and pollen plants.

- Larvae and adults feed on grasshopper eggs, cucumber beetles, aphids, and moth larvae.

- Attract soldier beetles by growing nectar and pollen plants, such as goldenrod, milkweed, and hydrangeas. (Soldier beetle adults will congregate in large numbers on these plants.)

- You can also attract soldier beetles by maintaining undisturbed areas near your vegetable garden.

-- SPIDER MITE DESTROYER -------------

Adults look like small, shiny, black lady beetles with white fuzzy hairs. Spider mite destroyer larvae look like dark gray, segmented, stubby little worms. Destroyer eggs are white and are laid singly in spider mite webs.

- Both adults and larvae feed on spider mites, which are tiny and attack most vegetables.

Spider mite destroyers will take care of spider mite problems for you if you invite them in with plants from the mustard or carrot families.

- Attract spider mite destroyers by growing a variety of pollen and nectar plants from the carrot and mustard families. These include plants such as Queen-Anne's-lace, parsley, parsnips, and radishes (be sure to let the plants flower to supply pollen and nectar).

Although tachinid flies look like houseflies, they're actually good guys who parasitize a variety of pest caterpillars.

TACHINID FLIES

Adults look like large, dark, bristly houseflies. They lay live, maggotlike larvae in pest insects.

- Tachinid fly larvae are parasites of squash bugs, corn borers, cutworms, Japanese beetles, and many pest caterpillars, including gypsy moth caterpillars.

- Tachinid flies are important natural suppressors of tent caterpillar and armyworm outbreaks.

- Attract tachinid flies by growing plants from the carrot family, such as Queen-Anne's-lace, and other small-flowered plants, such as sweet alyssum and spearmint.

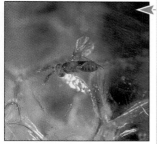

If you grow plants to attract trichogramma wasps, make sure to include some tall plants, such as sunflowers, for shelter.

TRICHOGRAMMA WASPS

Adult trichogramma wasps are very tiny; most are less than $1/50$ of an inch long. They're often yellow, or yellow and black, with bright red eyes.

- These pencil-point-size wasps parasitize more than 200 species of moth eggs, including cabbage and corn pests.

- Attract the wasps by growing pollen and nectar flowers, such as Queen-Anne's-lace, goldenrod, and milkweed. Fava beans and vetch (a versatile winter legume) are welcome attractions for these good guys, too.

- Also attract these wasps by planting vegetables such as broccoli and radishes and letting them flower.

- Provide shelter for trichogramma wasps by planting tall plants, such as sunflowers, in your garden.

BIG-EYED BUGS

Adult big-eyed bugs are ⅛ to ¼ inch long; are gray, brown, black, or tan with tiny black spots; and have very large eyes. Eggs are laid singly on leaves near potential prey. Adults and nymphs both drop to the ground when disturbed.

Big-eyed bugs have their big eyes out for a host of pests, including corn earworms and aphids.

- Adults eat aphids, mites, thrips, tarnished plants bugs, Mexican bean beetle eggs, and corn earworms, just to name a few.

- Attract big-eyed bugs by growing pollen and nectar plants (especially sweet alyssum, alfalfa, and goldenrod).

- Provide shelter by letting some weedy areas remain undisturbed.

GROUND BEETLES

These large, dark-color beetles are fast-moving and have long legs. Most are nocturnal, seeking shelter under rocks or garden debris in the daytime. Ground beetle larvae are long, tapered, segmented, and usually dark-colored.

To encourage ground beetles to take up residence, try creating a permanent planting of perennials near your vegetable garden.

- Both adults and larvae eat snails and slugs, caterpillars, cutworms, root maggots, and armyworms, and the eggs, larvae, and pupae of the Colorado potato beetle.

- Attract ground beetles by growing pollen-providing plants such as goldenrod and yarrow.

- Provide moist shelter by planting dense cover crops, leaving some tall weeds such as goldenrod and wild amaranth, and by creating a permanent planting of perennials near your vegetable garden.

Familiar lady beetles are powerful garden allies that eat aphids and many other kinds of pests.

LADY BEETLES

Often called ladybugs, most lady beetles are shorter than ½ inch long and vary widely in coloring and markings; some are red or orange with 12 black spots, others are pink with black spots, while still others are all black or all gray. Larvae are tiny, sometimes with bright orange or bright red markings.

- Lady beetle adults and larvae eat aphids; some also feed on scale insects, Colorado potato beetle eggs and larvae, mealybugs, European corn borer eggs, and spider mites.

- Attract these beetles by planting pollen and nectar plants, especially dill, dandelion, wild carrot, angelica, cosmos, goldenrod, yarrow, and sunflowers.

- To provide overwintering sites, plant some perennials in or near your vegetable garden.

- Stagger corn plantings so pollen is always available.

Green lacewings may be tiny, but they can do serious damage to leafhopper and Mexican bean beetle populations.

GREEN LACEWINGS

Green lacewing adults are bright green, about ¾ inch long with golden eyes and four large, lacy wings. Their larvae (also known as aphid lions) are about ¾ inch long and are pinkish brown and cream in color. Adults fly at night.

- Lacewing larvae eat aphids, mealybugs, mites, leafhoppers, and Mexican bean beetle eggs.

- Attract green lacewings by growing dill, caraway, angelica, cosmos, dandelions, sunflowers, sweet alyssum, and goldenrod in or near your garden.

KEEPING THEM OUT AND STICKING THEM UP

It may take several years until your garden has a substantial population of beneficial insects. Once they're established, beneficial insects may do all your pest control for you. But until they are, you'll want to try some of these special techniques for stopping pest problems before they get started.

Floating Row Covers

Row covers are pieces of lightweight synthetic fabric that are especially useful for keeping mobile pests, including cabbage moths (which beget cabbageworms), Colorado potato beetles, most aphids, and Mexican bean beetles, away from crops.

Cover your vegetables with row cover early in the season, when they're just young seedlings. If the crop you're protecting doesn't require insect pollination (such as potatoes, lettuce, and carrots), you can keep the covers on all season if you want to. If the crop needs insects to visit its flowers in order to set fruit (such as tomatoes, squash, and eggplant), you'll need to remove the covers when those flowers open. See "Floating Row Covers" on page 9 for more information.

Sticky Traps

Color is key with sticky traps, which are made of a rigid material coated with a sticky substance. Sticky traps are used to catch bad bugs that are attracted to a particular color. Yellow traps, for example, attract whiteflies and winged aphids. White traps lure whiteflies, cucumber beetles, and flea beetles. One precaution: Don't put out sticky traps unless you're sure you have a problem with a particular insect that will be attracted to the traps, because sticky traps also lure and trap beneficial insects. If you put them out randomly, you may be doing your garden more harm than good.

quick tip

Handheld vacuums work well for automatically handpicking pest insects. Remember to empty the vacuumed pests into a bucket of soapy water to kill them, or they may simply crawl out of the vacuum and find their way back to your plants.

Make sure you have a problem with a particular insect before resorting to sticky traps, so you don't end up trapping beneficial insects.

You can buy packaged sticky traps or you can make your own. Here's how:

1. Using scissors, cut plastic insulation board of an appropriate color into 4 x 6-inch pieces.

2. Cover each trap with a plastic sandwich bag.

3. Coat each bag with a commercial vegetable-based sticky substance, like Tangle-Trap.

4. Hang the traps close to the plant at plant height, at about 3- to 5-foot intervals.

5. Once the traps are covered with bugs, remove the plastic bag, wrap the trap with a new plastic bag, and coat it with more sticky stuff.

FIGHTING PESTS WITH SPRAYS

Every once in a while, one of your crops may be hit by a serious pest problem. When that happens, you'll probably need to intervene and kill the pests quickly to save your crop. Two substances you can use safely are insecticidal soap and BT (*Bacillus thuringiensis*).

Insecticidal Soap

You can spray plants with insecticidal soap to kill soft-bodied insects such as aphids and whiteflies. To be effective, the soap solution must come in contact with the bad bugs while it's still liquid—it has no effect after it dries on the plant.

Soaps may also damage plants if the plants are drought- or heat-stressed, or if you apply too much of the spray. As a precaution, spray some soap on a few leaves of each type of plant you want to treat, and then wait 48 hours. If the leaves are fine, you can go ahead and spray the entire plant.

You can buy a concentrated commercial insecticidal soap and dilute it according to the instructions on the label, or you can make your own by mixing 1 to 3 teaspoons of household dish soap (not detergent) with a gallon of water. You can apply insecticidal soap using a hand-pump spray bottle.

Bacillus Thuringiensis (BT)

Bacillus thuringiensis (BT) is a naturally occurring bacterium found in soil. When this bacteria infects caterpillars, it produces a toxin that kills the caterpillars. The bacterium does not affect humans or any other animals except caterpillars.

The BT strain most commonly used by home gardeners is *B. thuringiensis* var. *kurstaki*, which kills hundreds of different kinds of pest caterpillars, including cabbageworms. *B. thuringiensis* var. *tenebrionis* kills Colorado potato beetles.

Most forms of BT are sold as a liquid or powder that you dilute with water and then spray on the plants you want to protect. Here are some things to keep in mind when you use BT:

- BT is usually effective only against the larval stage of pest insects, so you must time your applications carefully. As soon as you spot the pest larvae, thoroughly coat the affected plants with BT.

- BT does kill caterpillars of desirable insects such as monarch butterflies, so don't spray it randomly. Be careful to aim the spray only at the plants that are infested with pest caterpillars.

quick tip

If you buy commercial insecticidal soap and have hard water, use bottled drinking water instead of your hard water to mix up the soap. The minerals in hard water interfere with the insecticidal action of the soap and may make the spray more likely to cause leaf damage.

Protect vegetables like zucchini from being damaged by aphids by spraying these bad guys with insecticidal soap.

(they're actually mollusks), but these notorious slimers can cause as much trouble in your vegetable garden as the most determined insect pest. Slugs are most damaging in wet years or regions, and they attack almost any tender plant. They hang out under rocks, garden debris, and mulches during the day. At night, they emerge and chew large, ragged holes in plant leaves and stems.

Slugs like yeast, so set out shallow pans of beer buried with the container lip flush to the soil surface. Once the slugs fall in the pan, they can't get out. To keep slugs out of the garden, you can edge your beds with 4- to 8-inch strips of copper flashing. Or place some boards around the perimeter of your garden; check the undersides of the boards each morning and destroy the slugs that have collected there.

4 GARDEN BAD GUYS

When you discover insects on your vegetable plants, take time to figure out what they are before you decide to kill them. For one thing, they may well be beneficial insects that don't need to be controlled at all! Plus, unless you know what pest you're fighting, you won't know what control method will work best.

Four of the most common vegetable garden insect pests are aphids, imported cabbageworms, Colorado potato beetles, and cucumber beetles. These pests attack more than one kind of crop and they can be problematic in almost any part of the United States. If you have a problem with a pest on a specific crop, and the description of the pest *doesn't* match one of those below, try looking up the crop in "Vegetable Favorites," beginning on page 65. You'll find extra information on crop-specific pests there.

Aphids

Description: Aphids are tiny, pear-shaped, green, pink, black, or dusty gray insects that cluster on plants.

Damage: Aphids suck plant sap, which causes plants to be stunted and distorted. Sooty mold often grows on sticky honeydew that the aphids secrete. Aphids attack most vegetables.

Controls: Spray plants frequently with a strong stream of water to knock aphids off, or spray insecticidal soap.

Imported Cabbageworms

Description: These pests are velvety green caterpillars with a fine yellow stripe down their backs.

Damage: Imported cabbageworms eat large ragged holes in leaves and soil plants with dark green droppings. Cabbageworms attack cabbage-family crops, including broccoli.

Controls: Handpick the caterpillars. To prevent damage, cover small plants with floating row covers immediately after planting.

Colorado Potato Beetles

Description: Colorado potato beetles are yellowish orange beetles with ten lengthwise black stripes on their wing covers. The larvae are orange, hump-backed grubs with black spots on their sides.

Damage: Adults and larvae chew the leaves on eggplants, potatoes, and tomatoes.

Controls: To prevent beetles from reaching the plants, cover plants with floating row cover from planting time until mid-season. Try mulching plants with a deep layer of straw.

One easy way to control Colorado potato beetles is by picking them off your plants.

It's easy to control this pest by handpicking the adults and larvae off the plants whenever you see them and drowning them in a jar of hot soapy water. If that isn't sufficient, you can also spray plants with *Bacillus thuringiensis* var. *tenebrionis*.

Cucumber Beetles

Description: These beetles are yellow or greenish yellow with black spots or stripes on their wing covers.

Damage: Cucumber beetles feed on leaves and blossoms, while their larvae feed on roots. Beetles and larvae attack squash-family crops.

Controls: Pile deep straw mulch around plants. Remove and destroy spent plants after harvest. Plant varieties that tolerate cucumber beetles.

FOUR-FOOTED FOES

Those wild neighbors with four feet can wreak a lot of havoc in midnight raids on your garden. But you can put a damper—if not a complete end—to their munching. You just have to tailor your game plan to the specific animal pest.

Raccoons

These cuddly looking creatures enjoy sweet corn—and lots of it. You'll know that a raccoon has visited your garden if ears of corn are stripped clean or gone entirely and cornstalks are bent to the ground.

The best raccoon barrier is an electric fence with two strands of wire—one at 6 inches and the other at 12 inches above the ground. Use fiberglass posts—raccoons can easily scale a wooden one. (Be sure you follow all of the manufacturer's safety instructions before installing the fence.)

Prevent rabbits from making a meal out of your garden by spreading deterrents, such as black or cayenne pepper, around your plants.

Rabbits

Rabbits relish carrots, peas, beans, lettuce, and beets. They usually nibble plants cleanly and level them right to the ground. The best rabbit barrier is a fence of 1-inch mesh chicken wire. You'll need to buy a roll of wire wide enough so that you can bury at least 6 inches of it in the ground, keep at least 2 feet of it above ground, *and* turn several inches outward at the top to act as a baffle. Other methods used to repel Benjamin Bunny include spreading deterrents such as black pepper, cayenne pepper, or bloodmeal around your plants.

Deer

Deer crave corn and most other vegetables. To repel deer, you can try hanging strongly scented soap or old panty hose filled with human or dog hair around the garden. The best defense against deer, though, is electric fencing. String wire 2½ feet high and add strips of masking tape smeared with peanut butter every 3 feet. Cover the peanut butter strips with flaps of aluminum foil to make it more noticeable to the deer. Deer sample the treat and get zapped for their efforts—which discourages them from visiting your veggies.

Groundhogs

These critters deserve being called "hogs." They will devour almost anything in the garden, including peas, beans, lettuce, and squash. You can protect young seedlings with row covers, or try sprinkling black pepper, cayenne pepper, or bloodmeal on your crops. The surest defense is to put up a wire mesh fence with at least 10 to 12 inches of wire belowground (preferably 18 to 24 inches) and a floppy baffle of wire at the top—groundhogs can dig *and* climb!

Gophers

Gophers go mostly for root vegetables (carrots, garlic, radishes, potatoes, and such). Because gophers are such prodigious diggers, you've got to bury a fence deep enough to stop them. Use hardware cloth and bury it at least 18 inches deep; your fence only needs to be 6 to 12 inches aboveground. You can also try encircling your vegetable garden with gopher-repelling plants such as *Euphorbia lathyris* (sold commercially as "Nature's Farewell Seed") or oleander.

FOR THE BIRDS

BIRDS CAN BE A MILD nuisance or a major pest in home gardens. You can scare birds by fooling them into thinking their enemies are present. Try placing inflatable, solid, or silhouetted likenesses of snakes, hawks, or owls strategically around your garden to discourage birds (and small mammals, too). They'll be most effective if you occasionally reposition them so that they appear to move about the garden.

Unusual noises can also frighten birds. Try fastening aluminum pie plates to stakes with strings in and around your garden.

And don't forget two tried-and-true methods: making a scarecrow and keeping Fido or Kitty on your property.

The payoff for your labor in the garden is rich: a bounty of luscious, fresh-tasting vegetables.

Vegetable Favorites

Buying tomatoes from the store doesn't quite compare to going out to your garden and picking a fresh, juicy love apple off the vine and sinking your teeth into it right then and there. In this chapter, we'll tell you how to grow tomatoes and many other vegetables. We'll also give you some tips on disease control and harvesting hints so that you get the most out of the fruits of your labor.

Growing your own vegetables is fun, relaxing, and can offer rewards practically year-round. In spring, you can taste the first offerings of the season, as your garden produces early birds such as peas, lettuce, broccoli, and spinach.

By the time summer rolls around your garden will be in full force, bursting with tomatoes, peppers, cucumbers, zucchini, carrots, beets, sweet corn, and anything else your heart (or taste buds!) desires. And not only is summer prime time for eating fresh vegetables, it's also a chance to preserve some of summer's bounty, whether it be by canning, freezing, drying, or making jelly or jam.

The arrival of fall doesn't necessarily mean the end of your garden's goodness. After all, some crops, such as carrots and broccoli, love cool weather. Fall is a chance to stretch the growing season just a little bit longer, before Old Man Winter knocks on the door. And once he does, it's time to open that jar of tomatoes you canned back in July.

Winter also gives you a chance to start thinking about next year's garden. What vegetables do you want to definitely grow again? What new ones do you want to try? Do you want to plant more zucchini, or less?

Before you know it, you'll be back outside, digging in the dirt and loving every minute of it.

> **Growing a vegetable garden can offer rewards practically year-round.**

BEANS

Beans are one of the easiest vegetables to grow, which makes them perfect for a children's garden.

Growing Tips

- **Soil preparation:** Beans prefer light soil with good drainage, so work in lots of compost. If your garden has heavy soil or poor drainage, you may want to build raised beds (see "Building Raised Beds" on page 20).

- **Planting:** Unlike peas, beans like warmer temperatures, so begin planting your bean crop about two weeks after the last frost. The soil temperature should be at least 60°F. (If the soil is too moist and cold, the seeds will rot.)

- **Spacing:** Sow your seeds about 1 to 2 inches apart in rows 18 to 30 inches apart, then thin the seedlings to about 6 inches apart.

- **Watering:** Water your soil before you plant to increase germination. Once the seedlings emerge, give them 1 inch of water a week, keeping the soil moist.

- **Fertilizing:** If you added compost before planting, your beans should be fine throughout the season.

- **Special hints:** To get a head start on warming the soil, cover it with black plastic as soon as you can work the soil in spring. Plant through holes poked in the plastic.

You can make a bean teepee to support pole beans—all you need are some wooden poles and strong nylon cord. For specific directions, see "Building a Bean Teepee" on the opposite page.

Pest Watch

- Skeletonized leaves are the work of Mexican bean beetles. Adults are small, yellowish brown beetles with black spots on their wing covers. Larvae are fat, yellowish orange grubs with long, branching spines. Cover young bean plants with floating row covers and handpick adults and larvae daily. In the fall, make sure to pull and destroy all bean plants.

- Aphids are also frequent visitors to beans. For how to control them, see "Fighting Pests the Organic Way" on page 51.

Disease Alert

- Beans are susceptible to rust, which looks like small, reddish brown circles on the undersides of leaves. Control this fungus by spraying the leaves with sulfur at the first sign of the disease, and repeat every 10 to 14 days as needed.

- If your bean leaves are mottled with golden yellow and are crinkled or curled, your plants may be suffering from bean mosaic virus. There is no cure for infected plants, so you should pull out and destroy them to protect plants that aren't infected.

- Powdery white patches on pods (which may be stunted) are signs of powdery mildew. Thin plants to promote air circulation, and handle the plants only when the foliage is dry.

Harvest Hints

Green beans are ready to pick when they are about the width of a pencil. The pods should snap when you break them in half. Use your thumb and fingernails to pinch beans off plants; yanking or tugging at the pods will damage stems and plant roots. Store green beans in plastic bags in the refrigerator. They will keep for one to two weeks; surplus beans can and freeze well.

BUILDING A BEAN TEEPEE

POLE BEANS REQUIRE some kind of support for their twining vines. Supports ensure that the plants get enough light and air to stay healthy. One type of support you can build for beans is a bean teepee.

1. Lash two 8- to 10-foot wooden poles together with strong nylon cord about 6 to 9 inches away from one end of the poles. Then bind on more poles one at a time, using a figure-eight pattern. Use six to eight poles total.

2. Stand the poles up and spread them to form a teepee. Push the poles several inches into the soil. Poke planting holes in the soil around the poles. Plant six to eight pole bean seeds in a hill around each pole.

3. After the bean seedlings begin to form true leaves, thin them to three plants per hill. The vines will climb the poles and cover the teepee, creating an attractive garden feature.

CAULIFLOWER

THE SWEET, MILD TASTE of garden-fresh cauliflower is well worth the little bit of extra attention this veggie needs. Growing conditions for cauliflower are similar to those of broccoli, although you can put your cauliflower transplants out when it's a little cooler—when daytime temperatures are above 50°F.

Unless you grow a self-blanching type of cauliflower (or a purple or green-headed type), you'll need to shield cauliflower heads from the sun to keep them white. When the heads are egg-size, fasten the leaves around the head with soft twine or raffia. (The leaves and heads must be dry when you wrap them.) The head will reach harvestable size in 2 to 14 days, depending on temperatures. Unwrap the heads to check growth, or after a heavy rain to let them dry out.

Harvest cauliflower heads when they're solid, and store them wrapped in plastic in the refrigerator up to a week.

BROCCOLI

This nutritious garden classic tastes great whether it's served raw or cooked.

Growing Tips

- **Soil preparation:** Broccoli likes a sunny location with good drainage, so dig in lots of compost or well-rotted manure.

- **Planting:** Plant broccoli transplants in the garden when both the soil and the air outside have warmed up to 55° to 60°F.

- **Spacing:** Space the plants 15 to 18 inches apart in rows that are 2 to 3 feet apart.

- **Watering:** Broccoli needs a regular supply of moisture to produce good heads, but it does not like excessive moisture. In fact, if the plants get too much water, they'll become stunted and die.

- **Fertilizing:** When they begin to form heads, feed the plants with compost tea or fish emulsion to help maximize their spear production.

- **Special hints:** Limit fungal diseases by growing broccoli and other brassica family vegetables (such as cabbage and cauliflower) only once every three years in the same plot.

Pest Watch

- Large, ragged holes in broccoli leaves are the work of cabbage loopers. These green caterpillars have two white lines down their backs and hatch from eggs laid by adult moths on leaf undersides. Handpick the loopers several times a week, or spray the larvae with *Bacillus thuringiensis* var. *kurstaki*.

- Plants that wilt at midday or become stunted may be infested with cabbage maggots. The white, tapering, 1/4-inch maggots bore into plant roots. Cover seedlings

with floating row covers, burying the edges in the soil. Burn or destroy seriously infected plants; also burn or destroy roots when harvesting tops.

Disease Alert

Your broccoli heads can fall victim to fungal rot, which turns the head centers black or discolored. This happens when water collects between the individual flower buds, so water from below. Cold weather can also cause the heads to turn black; try to protect your plants with a row cover if temperatures are forecast to sink below 40°F.

Harvest Hints

Broccoli heads are actually a cluster of immature flower buds, so be sure to harvest your broccoli when the heads are compact and the buds are still tightly closed. Cut off the main head of the broccoli at the stem using a sharp knife; cut at an angle so that water will run off the stem. Continue to water and feed your broccoli plants after cutting the main head, and you'll be rewarded with more cuttings of small but tasty heads that sprout and grow along the stem.

quick tip

Brussels sprouts, a relative of broccoli, matures from the base of the stem upwards. You can either pick the sprouts as you need them or harvest the whole stem. Brussels sprouts keep well in the refrigerator for up to three weeks, either on the stem or individually.

Your broccoli will be less susceptible to fungal diseases if you grow it and other vegetables from the same family, such as cabbage, only once every three years in the same plot.

quick tip

When planting cucumbers, scatter radish seed over the planting area. When allowed to flower, radishes seem to repel pests.

CUCUMBERS

Fresh cucumbers add zest to summer salads and crunch to sandwiches and are great for pickling. They're also a really easy vegetable to grow, making them a garden favorite.

Growing Tips

- **Soil preparation:** Cucumbers like well-drained, fertile soil that's been amended with lots of compost.

- **Planting:** Sow cucumber seeds in the ground when all danger of frost has passed. Both the soil and air temperature should be at least 60°F.

- **Spacing:** Place the seeds about 12 inches apart in rows that are 3 feet apart.

- **Watering:** Don't forget to water your cucumbers regularly. They like continuous moisture, and if they don't get it, you're at risk of producing bitter cucumbers. Don't worry if the plant's leaves wilt during the day; just make sure they recover at night. If they don't, you either aren't watering enough or they have a disease problem.

- **Fertilizing:** If you added compost to your soil before planting, you shouldn't have to feed your cucumbers during the growing season.

- **Special hints:** Try growing your cucumbers on a trellis. A trellis takes up less garden space and gives the plants more light.

Pest Watch

- Cucumber leaves and blossoms with holes in them have been munched by cucumber beetles.

Cucumbers mature quickly, so make sure to check your garden every day for cukes that are ready to pick.

These pests are ¼-inch-long, yellow or greenish yellow beetles with black stripes or spots. Cover seedlings with floating row covers and pile deep straw mulch around plants. Or plant nonbitter varieties, which deter the beetles.

- Wilted vines that don't recover at night may be infested with squash vine borers. These pests are flat, white, 1-inch-long larvae that burrow into cucumber vines. Cover vines with floating row covers early in the season. You can also slit the affected stem, kill the borer, and cover the stem with moist soil to promote root growth.

- Cukes are also affected by aphids, which yellow and curl the leaves. To learn about controlling aphids, see "4 Garden Bad Guys" on page 60.

Disease Alert

- Fruit and leaves are both susceptible to bacterial wilt. This disease causes the vines to wilt at midday, starting with the younger leaves, and it causes the fruit to shrivel. You can try to control the spread of this disease by controlling cucumber beetles—they spread bacterial wilt.

- Cucumbers are also targets of downy mildew. Symptoms of this disease include yellow spots on the tops of leaves and purple to gray mold on the undersides. To prevent outbreaks, space plants to encourage air circulation and water them early in the day.

Harvest Hints

The key to harvesting cucumbers is to do so continuously. They mature very quickly and if you leave them on the vine too long they'll get huge. To pick cucumbers, hold the stem with one hand and pull the fruit with the other. After you've picked them, refrigerate immediately. Be sure not to wash the cucumbers until you are ready to use them.

CHOOSING CUKES

BURPLESS? NONBITTER? Slicers? Picklers? What's the difference between these cucumbers?

Burpless varieties don't form the chemical compounds that cause people to burp. Most burpless cukes are long-fruited oriental types that produce lots of cucumbers.

Nonbitter varieties don't form the bitter compounds that can develop in the fruits of drought-stressed plants. The absence of these chemicals in the leaves also deters cucumber beetles.

Slicing cucumbers are those dark green cukes that most people think of when they think of cucumbers. You can make pickles with young slicing cucumbers, but if you want to make a lot of pickles, plant a pickling variety, which will produce smaller fruits than young slicers.

Harvesting peas daily will help keep the plants productive. You can refrigerate fresh peas for up to one week.

PEAS

Eating peas fresh from the garden is just like eating candy—once you've had a taste, you'll keep coming back for more.

Growing Tips

- **Soil preparation:** Peas grow best in loose, well-drained soil. Work lots of compost into the soil before planting.

- **Planting:** Peas grow best when the air temperature is 60° to 65°F. Sow pea seed as soon as the ground can be worked in spring and the soil temperature reaches 40°F.

- **Spacing:** Sow seeds 1 to 2 inches apart with 18 inches between rows. When the plants are 2 to 3 inches tall, thin them to 2 to 3 inches apart.

- **Watering:** Peas thrive in cool, moist soil. So keep it consistently moist but not soggy.
- **Fertilizing:** If you added compost before planting your peas, they should be fine.
- **Special hints:** Put up a trellis or other support before planting, at planting time, or when the seedlings are a few inches tall.

Pest Watch

- If your plants have small notches cut out of their leaves, they may be the victims of pea leaf weevils. Weevils rarely cause serious damage unless plants are small. In the future, cover plants with floating row covers until they are at least 1 foot tall.
- If the leaves are yellow and distorted, you could have tarnished plant bugs or pea aphids. (See "4 Garden Bad Guys" on page 60 for tips on controlling aphids.) Tarnished plant bugs are oval, light green or brown, 1/4-inch-long bugs, and you can fight them with white sticky traps.

Disease Alert

- Bacterial blight can give your pea leaves light brown to purple spots and can even spread to the pods. Destroy any infected plants and collect and destroy all spent plant material after harvest.
- Fusarium wilt causes pea leaves to yellow and the plant to die. Pull out and destroy infected plants. In the future, plant in raised beds.

Harvest Hints

When the pods are plump and the peas are just touching, it's time to pick. You don't want to leave the peas on the plants too long because they'll get starchy. Hold the plant with one hand and pull the peas off gently.

POPULAR PEAS

YOU CAN GROW a lot of different kinds of peas in your garden, such as:

Snow peas. Snow peas produce tender, succulent pods that you can eat raw or add to cooked dishes such as stir-fries. Harvest them when the pods are young and flat and the seeds are small and immature.

Snap peas. These peas bear tender pods with juicy seeds, both of which are edible. Pick when the pods are plump and bulging with mature seeds. Snap peas are delicious raw or cooked.

Dry peas. Dry peas are grown for their seeds. Harvest them when the pods have turned brown. Shell the peas, then spread them out to dry for three weeks. Add them to soups, or just use them like dried beans.

PEPPERS

Peppers come in all sizes, shapes, colors, and flavors—from sweet bell peppers to hot habaneros that will light up your mouth. And they're easy to grow. Peppers are great in salsas and stir-fries, or grilled, stuffed, or pickled (Peter Piper's favorite).

Growing Tips

- **Soil preparation:** Choose a well-drained site that gets at least eight hours of sunlight a day. Peppers need more fertile soil than most vegetables, so add lots of compost. They won't do well, however, if they get too much nitrogen (you'll just get lots of leaves and not many peppers). If your soil is lacking in phosphorous, add some rock phosphate or bonemeal before planting.

- **Planting:** Plant your seedlings after the threat of spring frost and when the soil has reached at least 65°F.

Although you can eat most peppers when they're green, they don't develop their full flavor until they've turned color—in this case, from green to red.

- **Spacing:** Dig your peppers' planting holes about 18 inches apart to let sunlight in.

- **Watering:** Peppers like moist soil, but they won't stand for wet feet, so be careful not to overwater them. (They tolerate drought better than tomatoes or eggplants do.)

- **Fertilizing:** After the flowers have turned into baby peppers, sidedress a balanced organic fertilizer such as compost around the base of the plants.

- **Special hints:** In hot climates, shade peppers by planting them in the shadow of taller crops, such as corn or trellised beans, or by planting them in a dense block to help protect the fruit from bright afternoon sun.

Pest Watch

- If your pepper plants have been chewed off at the stems, chances are you have cutworms. Cutworms are fat, greasy-looking, gray or dull brown, 1- to 2-inch caterpillars with shiny heads. To protect against these pests, place paper collars—made from empty, cut-up toilet paper or paper towel rolls—around the seedlings after planting.

- Holes in blossoms or buds that result in mutated fruit are the work of pepper weevils. These beetles are brass-colored with a brown or black snout. Collect and destroy all dropped and damaged flower buds and fruit. Control pepper weevils by keeping your garden free of debris and by handpicking any beetles you see.

- Aphids are also frequent visitors to peppers. For how to control them, see "4 Garden Bad Guys" on page 60.

A PEPPER FIESTA

YOU CAN HARVEST an exciting mixture of tastes, shapes, and colors from backyard pepper plants. Here's a look at the different types.

Sweet Peppers

Bell peppers. Often called green peppers, these sweet-tasting, blocky peppers have thick walls.

Frying or salad peppers. These peppers tend to be longer than they are wide and have thinner walls than bell peppers do. Frying peppers have a mellow flavor.

Pimiento peppers. These peppers are thick-walled, heart-shaped, and very sweet when ripe.

Hot Peppers

Chile peppers. Chile peppers have long or triangular fruits only an inch or two wide.

Small hot peppers. Often, the smaller the pepper, the hotter its fire. Long, skinny cayenne peppers are hot. Thumb-size jalapeños are hotter and widely used.

Disease Alert

- Verticillium and fusarium wilts sometimes affect peppers, yellowing the leaves at the bottom of the plant. The best defense against these diseases is to plant in well-drained soil and to water evenly. Raised beds give pepper roots a healthy edge against these diseases.

- Peppers are also affected by early blight, a leaf spot disease. You can identify blight by the dark, concentrically ringed spots that form on your pepper's leaves. To help reduce the amount of blight on your peppers, simply pluck the affected leaves off. Leaf blight won't seriously damage your peppers, and may not even affect yield.

Harvest Hints

You can eat most peppers when they're green, but they don't develop their full flavor until they turn color—whether it be red, orange, or yellow. Cut sweet peppers off the plant with a sharp knife or shears, leaving about a ½-inch stem attached. Cayennes and some others usually pop off with ample stems attached.

Peppers will usually keep in the refrigerator for up to two weeks. Freeze or dry any excess fruit.

Harvest all usable fruit before the first hard frost. Or, if you have unripe fruit you don't want to waste, cut the entire plant and hang it indoors to allow the fruit to continue ripening.

The blocky fruits of bell peppers are excellent for stuffing or just eating raw.

HEAVENLY HOT PEPPERS

SO YOU WANT to try your hand at growing peppers? Why not try some hot and spicy types to go along with your sweet peppers? Hot peppers are versatile and add zest to food. The question is, how much heat can you take? Check out the hot pepper rating scale (called the Scoville rating) to see where some chile peppers stand:

Pepper Type	Scoville Heat Units
Habanero	200,000–300,000
Tabasco	30,000–50,000
Chile pequin	40,000
Cayenne	35,000
Jalapeño	3,500–4,500
Bell	0

Follow the same growing conditions for hot peppers as you would for sweet peppers. Just remember to wear latex or rubber gloves when cutting up hot peppers—and don't touch your eyes. (If you do, flush them out with water.) Capsaicin, the compound in peppers that gives them their heat, is a powerful substance and can really burn. After you've finished cutting the peppers, throw the gloves away and wash your hands well with soap.

POTATOES

This delicious root crop is one of the most versatile vegetables. You can mash potatoes, bake them, slice them up and fry them, stuff them—the possibilities are almost endless. Plus, they're easy to grow, and you can store them for a long time after harvest.

Growing Tips

● **Soil preparation:** Potatoes love loose, sandy soil that's high in organic matter, so add lots of compost before planting.

● **Planting:** As long as your soil is dry, you can plant potatoes up to four weeks before the last expected spring frost.

Once your potatoes are ready to harvest, dig them up carefully. Then shake off excess dirt, and bring them indoors to dry.

● **Spacing:** Space potatoes about 10 to 14 inches apart. If you're going to harvest early (and therefore have smaller potatoes) you could crowd them 8 inches apart.

● **Watering:** This root crop likes consistently moist soil and will crack if the moisture content fluctuates a lot. To prevent cracking, water regularly, especially in dry weather. To help keep the soil moist, put a thick layer of mulch around your plants.

● **Fertilizing:** If grown in good soil, potatoes don't need any fertilizer.

But to help your spuds along, add a cup of compost to each plant a month after planting.

- **Special hints:** Mulching with straw reduces pest problems on potatoes and improves their yields. So after planting, don't hesitate to throw on some straw for the season.

Pest Watch

- Potato leaves full of holes signal the infamous Colorado potato beetle. For how to control them, see "Fighting Pests the Organic Way" on page 51.

- Potatoes that end up with small tunnels running through them have been attacked by flea beetle larvae. These thin, white, brown-headed grubs attack in early July. Keeping a thick mulch over the soil is a good way to prevent their destructive habits.

Disease Alert

- Early blight is a fungus that affects potato leaves and looks like brown spots formed in concentric rings. Remove the infected leaves before the fungus moves to your tubers and reduces your yield.

- Ring rot is a bacteria that infects the tubers and is hard to see aboveground. You might not notice it until you harvest the potatoes and only find a shell of firm tissue with a hollow center. The best way to prevent ring rot is to use certified disease-free seed and to wash your knife after cutting up each tuber for seeding.

- Another disease that affects potatoes is verticillium wilt, which turns older leaves yellow and eventually causes plants to die. Once your potatoes have this disease, the only option is to destroy infected plants to stop the disease from spreading (don't throw them on your compost pile!).

quick tip

You can get any potato spud to grow bigger a bit sooner if you let your potatoes sprout for two weeks before you plant them. Just keep them in a dark area at room temperature to begin with, and then move them to a well-lit area when they begin to sprout.

Harvest Hints

Potatoes are ready to harvest three weeks after the plants' first flowers bloom. For bigger, heartier potatoes, wait to dig until the aboveground green growth dies back at the end of the season. The ideal place to store your potatoes is a humid, dark spot that's about 35° to 45°F, such as a cellar, garage, or any unheated room.

TATERS IN CAGES

YOU CAN STILL GROW potatoes even if you don't have a lot of room. How? By growing them in a cage. Just follow these easy steps.

Form a circle out of chicken wire about 2 feet in diameter, and put 6 inches of soil and compost in the bottom. Place two or three potatoes on the soil and cover them with 4 more inches of soil and compost.

Wrap the entire container in burlap or an old sheet to block the sun. Each week for the next six weeks put another inch of soil and mulch on top. Water twice a week (if it doesn't rain) to keep the soil moist.

When the foliage dies, your potatoes are ready for harvest. All you have to do is dump out the container and collect your reward.

ROOT CROPS

Beets and carrots are two of the easiest vegetables you can grow as long as you take the time to prepare a fine, deep seedbed for them.

Growing Tips for Beets

- **Soil preparation:** Beets need well-drained sandy loam to perform their best. If you have heavy or poorly drained soil, build raised planting beds for your beets.

- **Planting:** Plant in early spring as soon as you can work the soil and soil temperatures exceed 45°F.

- **Spacing:** Space beets about 2 to 4 inches apart in rows that are 12 to 20 inches apart. When the plants are 2 to 3 inches tall, thin them to 4 to 6 inches apart.

- **Watering:** Keep beets consistently moist, not wet.

- **Fertilizing:** Once the first true leaves appear, feed your beets with compost tea. Repeat weekly until they're 2 to 3 inches tall.

- **Special hints:** If the enlarging roots poke up above the soil surface, hill up the soil to keep these "shoulders" from becoming green and tough.

Pest Watch

Leafminers can attack your beets and give the leaves curvy white, or translucent tunnels. To control these pale green, maggotlike larvae, pick off and destroy damaged leaves.

One key to growing tasty beets is consistent moisture. If you let the roots dry out, they'll become cracked, stringy, and tough.

Disease Alert

Curly top virus can affect your beet leaves, making them look stunted and crinkled. This disease can also affect the roots, making the flesh woody. If your potatoes have these symptoms, destroy the infected plants. Help avoid this virus by covering seedbeds with row covers after planting.

Harvest Hints

Beets are a good size to harvest when their roots are 1½ to 3 inches in diameter. Pull the roots out carefully so you don't bruise them, and cut off the green tops to about 1 inch from the root. You can refrigerate beets for several weeks.

Growing Tips for Carrots

● **Soil preparation:** Carrots do best in loose, moderately rich soil.

Before harvesting all of your carrots, pull out a few roots to check their size. If the ground's dry, watering before harvesting will make pulling them out of the ground easier.

- **Planting:** Same as beets.

- **Spacing:** Sow about six seeds per inch in rows 16 to 30 inches apart. When the carrots are about 2 inches tall, thin them to 1 inch apart. Two weeks later, thin them to 3 to 4 inches apart.

- **Watering:** Uneven moisture can cause the roots to crack, so keep carrots consistently moist.

- **Fertilizing:** If your soil has lots of organic matter in it, your carrots won't need anything extra.

- **Special hints:** Carrots do very well planted in an area where legumes (beans, peas) were before, because of the extra nitrogen that these plants leave behind.

FUN FACT

Sixteenth-century Englishwomen used green carrot tops as decorations on hats or in their hair! Not only that, but the first carrots cultivated—over 1,000 years ago—were purple. It wasn't until about 400 years ago that Dutch breeders began developing orange carrots.

Pest Watch

White maggots or tunnels filled with brown, crumbly material are the work of carrot rust flies. In the future, protect crops with floating row covers from seeding to harvest.

Disease Alert

- Dark, yellow-bordered spots on leaves signal fungal leaf blight. To fight this fungal infection, pick off spotted leaves and spray foliage with fish emulsion to encourage new growth.
- Stunted, light yellow leaves and woody roots with tufts of white side roots are signs of aster yellows. Leafhoppers spread this disease; spray insecticidal soap to control them. Pull up and destroy all infected plants.

Harvest Hints

Harvest carrots as soon as they're big enough to eat. Carrots will keep in the refrigerator in a plastic bag for up to three months.

SALAD GREENS

The best-tasting salads start with fresh greens right from the garden, such as leaf or head lettuce or spinach. All are easy to grow and harvest and are a great way to start your garden off in spring.

Growing Tips for Leaf and Head Lettuce

- **Soil preparation:** Almost all lettuces like fluffy, well-composted soil, so add in lots of organic matter such as aged manure or compost.

- **Planting:** Lettuce loves cool weather, so you can plant the seeds directly in the garden two to four weeks before your last expected frost.

- **Spacing:** Scatter seeds over the bed and cover them with a thin layer of soil. Space rows about 15 inches apart. After the seeds sprout, thin them out so you have about 6 to 10 inches between plants.

- **Watering:** Lettuce needs about 1 inch of water each week to thrive and will wilt very quickly if it dries out.

- **Fertilizing:** Water the plants with compost tea or fish emulsion once a week until they're 4 inches tall.

- **Special hints:** Hot weather can make lettuce bolt and become bitter. To extend your growing season, plant lettuce between or under larger plants to shade it from strong sun.

Pest Watch

- The notorious cutworm may strike, cutting off your little seedlings at the soil line. So look for fat, 1- to 2-inch brown caterpillars in the soil near the bases of your plants. To prevent cutworms, place cardboard collars over seedlings.

Lettuce has shallow roots, so pull weeds carefully to avoid damaging the roots.

- If your plants are yellow and stunted or wilt during the day and recover at night, they're probably suffering from wireworms (yellow to reddish brown, slender, segmented worms up to 1½ inches long). To control these critters, avoid planting where sod was laid the year before.

Disease Alert

- Powdery mildew can affect your plants and give them a white, powdery coating. Infected leaves curl, turn yellow, and eventually die. Spray plants with a baking soda solution of 1 teaspoon per quart of water.

- If your plant has yellow or light green spots on it, you most likely have downy mildew. Downy mildew is a fungal disease that's common in warm, damp weather. You can eat undamaged leaves. In the future, leave more space between plants to promote air circulation.

Harvest Hints

Start harvesting the outer leaves of your leaf lettuce early to encourage new growth. If the weather is getting warmer and you think the lettuce is going to bolt, harvest the whole plants. Head lettuce is a little different from leaf lettuce in that you must wait for the head to mature. Heads are ready to harvest when they're firm and tight. Simply pull up the plant and cut the roots off right in the garden!

Because leaf lettuce wilts quickly, you should eat it soon after picking. To refrigerate leaf lettuce, first rinse it in cool water. Then shake off the excess water and seal the lettuce in a plastic bag with a moist paper towel.

Growing Tips for Spinach

- **Soil preparation:** Spinach likes light, well-drained soil, so work lots of compost into your beds.

- **Planting:** Sow spinach directly in the ground in early spring as soon as the soil temperature reaches 35°F.

- **Spacing:** Broadcast the seed in rows that are 1 to 3 feet apart. Once the seedlings emerge, thin them so they're about 4 inches apart.

- **Watering:** Keep the plants moist, but not wet.

- **Fertilizing:** Water weekly with fish emulsion until the plants are 3 inches tall.

- **Special hints:** To help speed up seed germination, soak your seeds in compost tea for 15 minutes to overnight before sowing them.

You can harvest spinach leaves when they're at least 3 inches long. Or cut the entire plant just below the ground.

Pest Watch

- If your spinach leaves have light-color tunnels or blotches running through them, they're most likely suffering from leaf-miner damage. The larvae of these insects are white, $1/8$-inch-long maggots. Handpick and destroy damaged leaves. In the future, protect plants with floating row covers from seeding until harvest.

- Leaves with numerous small, round holes are the work of flea beetles. These tiny black, brown, or bronze beetles jump like fleas when disturbed. Leaves with holes are edible. In the future, cover plants with floating row covers until they're well established.

Disease Alert

Downy mildew produces pale yellow spots on leaves. Remove and destroy affected plants. To reduce problems, thin plants and avoid wetting the leaves when watering.

Harvest Hints

Pick individual outside leaves when they're at least 3 inches long. Spinach can last up to a week in the refrigerator.

CHARD

SWISS CHARD is a salad green that grows well in cool weather and keeps producing until a hard freeze kills it. You can eat it raw or cook it like spinach.

Growing tips: Chard likes rich, well-drained soil in a sunny site. Sow seed two to four weeks before the last expected frost; you can sow successive plantings until late summer. Plant chard in rows about 1½ feet apart. Direct-sow seeds 1 to 3 inches apart, and thin them to 5 to 8 inches apart when the plants are 6 to 8 inches tall.

Pest watch: Flea beetles are small, shiny, black beetles that chew little holes through chard leaves. To help prevent these little menaces from taking over, cover plants with row covers as soon as the seedlings emerge.

Disease alert: Downy mildew produces pale yellow spots on leaves. Remove and destroy affected plants. To reduce problems, thin plants and avoid wetting the leaves when watering.

Harvest hints: Pick the outer leaves as soon as they're large enough. You can refrigerate chard for up to two weeks after you've picked it.

ALIEN-LOOKING CORN

THOSE UNAPPEALING whitish gray blobs growing on your corn ears aren't signs of an alien invasion. Those blobs are actually corn smut, which is caused by a fungus. Remove and destroy deformed ears anywhere on the plant as soon as you see them, and remove and destroy spent corn plants after harvest. What you do with that blob of smut, however, is your choice. You can destroy it—or you might want to use it in a soup for your next dinner party. That's because corn smut (also known as cuitlacoche or huittlacoche) is considered a delicacy in regions such as Mexico. In fact, some farmers grow corn smut purposely for gourmet markets. People who like corn smut say it has a smoky-sweet flavor that's a cross between corn and mushrooms. It's used in a variety of dishes from soups to casseroles.

SWEET CORN

Summer just isn't summer without sitting down to a plate of fresh corn on the cob. Eating sweet corn is like eating candy—once you've had your first taste of those sumptuous kernels, you'll keep coming back for more.

Growing Tips

- **Soil preparation:** Corn is a heavy feeder and likes soil that is rich and well drained. Accommodate your corn plants by adding lots of aged manure and compost to your soil.

- **Planting:** The warmer your soil, the better. You can plant the earliest corn about two weeks after the last spring frost date or when the soil temperature is over 50°F.

- **Spacing:** Plant seeds about 15 inches away from one another in rows that are about 2½ feet apart.

- **Watering:** Keep the soil evenly moist, but not wet. Never let young plants dry out, and supply plenty of water when tassels begin to appear on your plants. Water your plants around their bases; if you water from the top you might wash away a lot of pollen, which would decrease the number of ears you'd get.

- **Fertilizing:** When the first leaves poke up through the ground, water with compost tea, and repeat weekly for three to four weeks.

- **Special hints:** Wait to thin your corn until the plants are about 2 to 4 inches high. To avoid damaging surrounding plants, thin by cutting off extra seedlings at ground level.

Pest Watch

- To protect young corn transplants from being chewed off at the stems by cutworms (fat, greasy-

looking, gray, 1- to 2-inch caterpillars with shiny heads), firmly place a cardboard collar around the base of each seedling.

- Leaves with holes in them and ears with tunnels through them are signs of the corn earworm. This frequent visitor of corn is a 2-inch-long yellow, green- or brown-striped worm. To defend your corn against these nasty pests, squirt vegetable or mineral oil into the tip of each ear when the silk appears; the oil will drown the worms.

Disease Alert

If you notice mottled yellow-and-green leaves and the plants are stunted and bushy, your corn is probably suffering from maize dwarf mosaic. Pull out and destroy infected plants. In the future, plant resistant corn varieties and control aphids to prevent them from spreading the disease.

To test your corn to see if it's ready, pull back partway on the husk of an ear, and press on a kernel with your thumbnail. If milky liquid spurts out, the corn is ready to pick and eat.

Harvest Hints

Harvest your corn when the silks are brown and damp and the kernels are plump and tender. A good way to see if corn is ready is to pull back the husk of an ear part of the way and press on a kernel with your thumbnail. If milky liquid spurts out, you can pick the ears. Corn doesn't keep very long, so pick what you need and keep it refrigerated until you want to use it. (Better yet, pick it right before you're ready to cook it.) Can or freeze excess corn right after harvesting.

TOMATOES

A vegetable garden isn't complete without tomatoes. After all, tomatoes are easy to grow and nothing tastes quite as good as a fresh-picked, garden-ripe tomato. Tomatoes are incredibly versatile, dressing up everything from a basic sandwich to your grandmother's secret recipe for sauce. You can even make tomato jam!

Growing Tips

- **Soil preparation:** These veggies do best in loose, rich, well-drained soil, so make sure to work lots of compost into your beds before planting.

- **Planting:** Tomatoes like warm soil and don't tolerate frost, so wait until warm spring days arrive and soil temperatures reach above 60°F to plant.

- **Spacing:** Plant tomatoes deeply, so the lowest set of leaves is at soil level, and press the soil down gently. If you're going to stake your tomatoes, leave about 1 to 3 feet between the plants, and space your rows 3 feet apart. For tomatoes that aren't staked, space the plants 3 feet apart in rows 4 feet apart.

Tomatoes are ready to pick when they just begin to change from orange to red. Let them finish ripening at room temperature somewhere out of direct sunlight.

- **Watering:** Once all your plants are in the ground, water them well. To avoid problems with disease, water from the bottom and early in the day. Tomatoes need even moisture, though, so don't let your beds dry out. As you learned in "Managing Your Garden" (see page 35), one way to retain moisture in the soil (as well as block weeds) is to mulch. So once the tomato plants are established, apply a thick mulch of straw, grass clippings, or composted leaves. On windy days, protect the young plants with row covers or cloches.

- **Fertilizing:** As long as you've added compost to your beds before planting, you shouldn't need to add any other fertilizer for tomatoes.

- **Special hints:** Keep your plants growing for a few more weeks once the weather turns cooler by covering them with old blankets before the first expected fall frost. When fall temps are consistently below 60°F, pick all mature green fruits and let them ripen indoors.

Pest Watch

- To protect young tomato transplants from being chewed off at the stems by cutworms (fat, greasy-looking, gray, 1- to 2-inch caterpillars with shiny heads), firmly place a cardboard collar around the base of each seedling. (You can cut up empty toilet paper rolls to make the collars.)

- If you notice holes in the leaves of your tomato plants or big, fat, green caterpillars lolling on the plants, you're probably dealing with tomato hornworms. Get the better of these pests by hand-picking them off the plants each day. If you see a lot of young (small) hornworm caterpillars, spray them with *Bacillus thuringiensis* var. *kurstaki* every few days.

3 MAJOR TYPES

TOMATOES COME in three different major fruit types: slicing, cherry, and paste. Juicy **slicing tomatoes** are what you probably think of as the stereotypical tomato: a fruit either small, medium, or large in size that's perfect for slicing onto a sandwich or burger. Beefsteak tomatoes are a particularly large and juicy type of slicer.

Cherry tomatoes are those tiny tomatoes that are perfect for popping into your mouth for a snack, adding to a salad, or serving as an appetizer. They tend to be sweet and prolific.

You can use **paste tomatoes** (also known as pear, plum, saladette, Roma type, sauce, and Italian tomatoes) in salads and for slicing, but they're best for making sauce. These tomatoes are meatier and have fewer seeds and less juice than other tomatoes.

HOW DOES YOUR TOMATO GROW?

TOMATO PLANTS GROW in one of two ways. Some grow to a certain height and then flower and produce all their fruit within about two weeks; these are called *determinate* tomatoes. The other type keeps growing taller and producing flowers and fruit indefinitely (in frost-free climates) or until the first frost—this type is called *indeterminate*. Determinate tomatoes are great if you're planning on canning or making sauce because you'll have enough for processing all at once. Indeterminate tomatoes are great if you want a steady supply of tomatoes from summer into fall.

Some determinate tomato plants are compact and don't require much, if any, staking, while others need to be staked, caged, or trellised to hold up all the tomatoes they produce. Indeterminate tomato plants have long, sprawling vines that you'll have to keep off the ground to get the healthiest fruit.

- Curled-down leaves and small pink, green, or black insects on leaf undersides signal aphids. For how to control them, see "4 Garden Bad Guys" on page 60.

Disease Alert

- If you spot speckles on any leaves (especially lower leaves) during the growing season, pinch off the affected leaves to reduce problems with early blight, late blight, and other leaf spot diseases. Then spray the plants with compost tea. Even if your plants continue to suffer from blights and leaf spots, relax—they'll probably still produce plenty of tomatoes for you to pick.

- You may also notice a sunken, brownish black area at the blossom end of some of your tomatoes. This condition is called blossom-end rot, and it's caused by poor calcium uptake, which is related to an uneven supply of water. The tomatoes are still edible (just cut out the brown part). To prevent more fruits from being affected, make sure to deeply and evenly water the plants.

- At the end of the season, be sure to pull out and destroy or throw away (not on your compost pile, though) all of your tomato plants if they showed any signs of disease. Otherwise, the next season's crop may be infected by disease organisms that survive the winter sheltered in the debris of the old crop.

Harvest Hints

Pick tomatoes when they just begin to change from orange to red. Gently twist the fruit off while holding the vine, then let the tomatoes finish ripening at room temperature out of direct sunlight. Don't store them in your refrigerator because the cold temperature will cause them to lose flavor and texture.

GIVE YOUR PLANTS A LIFT

ONE OF THE KEYS to growing lots of healthy tomatoes is to get them up off the ground—in other words, growing them upward. The easiest way to accomplish this is to use cages or stakes and string. Here are some helpful tips for each method.

Make the most of stakes and string with the stake and weave method. Plant your seedlings 18 inches apart, then place a sturdy stake between every two plants. When the plants reach 6 inches tall, tie string to one stake, weave the string around two plants, wrap it around the next stake, then continue weaving and wrapping from plant to plant and stake to stake until you get back to the first stake. Repeat this with a fresh "weave level" every time the plants grow another 6 to 8 inches.

If you're using cages, those made of concrete reinforcing mesh wire or heavy-gauge galvanized steel wire work best for supporting tomato plants. Carefully put one cage over each transplant when you plant it out in the garden; for added support, you might want to drive two stakes into the ground on opposite sides of each cage and then secure the cage to the stakes with twine. Or, use 18-inch sections of metal coat hangers for anchors. Bend the sections in the center (so they look like croquet wickets), loop them over the bottom rungs of the cage, then drive them into the ground. At the end of the season, pull out the spent tomato plants and cages, and save the cages for next year.

ZUCCHINI

You're probably well aware of how productive this summer squash can be. Once it takes off, it just doesn't stop producing. You can do lots of things with zucchini, though—cook and serve it in casseroles, slice it up and add it to pancakes, or bake zucchini bread.

Growing Tips

- **Soil preparation:** Zucchini likes well-drained, fertile soil that's been amended with lots of compost.
- **Planting:** Plant seed outdoors when the soil temperature has reached 60°F—about a week after the last frost.
- **Spacing:** You want to give your squash a lot of room to spread out and grow. Plant them about 3 to 4 feet apart in rows 8 to 12 feet apart.
- **Watering:** Zucchini like consistently moist soil. To prevent problems with disease, always water from below.
- **Fertilizing:** Spray plants with compost tea two weeks after seedlings come up. Spray again in three weeks or when the first flowers appear.
- **Special hints:** If space is limited, put up a trellis for vertical support.

Pest Watch

Pale to brown blotches on leaves are the work of squash bugs. Squash bugs are brownish

When you harvest zucchini, use a very narrow-bladed knife to make a clean cut across the stem 1 inch up from the fruit.

black, ½-inch-long bugs; their larvae are whitish green with dark heads and legs. You can control these pests by hand-picking them off the plants.

Disease Alert

Powdery mildew may strike the plants, leaving whitish powdery spots on leaves that turn brown and dry. Pick and destroy badly infected leaves. Rinse leaf tops and bottoms thoroughly with water once a week to slow the spread of this disease.

Harvest Hints

Harvest zucchini when the fruits are still small—about 3 to 4 inches across or 4 to 6 inches long. You can store zucchini in the refrigerator for about a week.

FUN FACT

THE FRUIT OF THE ZUCCHINI IS NOT THE ONLY EDIBLE PART OF THE PLANT. YOU CAN ALSO PICK THE MALE FLOWERS (THE SMALLER ONES) JUST BEFORE THEY OPEN AND USE THEM IN SOUPS, STIR-FRIES, OR OMELETS.

OTHER SUMMER SQUASH

ZUCCHINIS AREN'T THE ONLY summer squash. Others include:

Lebanese squash. This squash even beats zucchini for productivity. It's bulbous in shape, pastel green in color, and unbelievably prolific. This squash is also more disease- and pest-tolerant than other summer squash.

Crooknecks. Yellow crooknecks are those old-fashion squash with curvy necks. They have a nutty flavor.

Pattypans. These scalloped or flower-shaped squashes have pretty yellow or light green fruits. Pattypans seem to hold up well after being cooked for a long time, making them ideal for squash-and-potato stew.

Your Seasonal Vegetable-Care Calendar

OBVIOUSLY, PLANTING vegetables in Florida isn't the same as planting them in Maine because of the climatic conditions. That's why before you even start planning your vegetable garden, you need to know what hardiness zone you live in.

A plant's ability to withstand a given climate is called its hardiness. The USDA has developed a Plant Hardiness Zone Map that divides North America into ten numbered climatic zones. Zone 1 is the coldest, and Zone 10 is the warmest. You can check which zone you live in by looking at the map on page 106.

This seasonal care calendar is based on gardening in Zones 5 and 6, which means you'll have to adapt it if you live in a different zone. For example, if you live in a colder zone, such as Zone 3, you'll need to push things off for a month or two (or maybe even three). Instead of starting spring broccoli seedlings at the end of February, start them at the end of March or April. If you live in a warmer zone, such as 9 or 10, you'll need to start things earlier than what's listed here because your garden will probably peter out from the summer heat by July.

JANUARY

Although the start of prime gardening season is still a few months away, here are a few things you can do now to prepare:

- Run your **Christmas tree** through a chipper/shredder to make mulch for your garden paths come spring.

- Look through **seed catalogs** to dream about what you want to plant. If you plan to start plants from seed, **order the seed now!**

- **Inventory** your garden supplies and make sure you have the essentials (such as row covers and plant cages); take a shopping trip or order from a catalog to buy items that are in short supply.

FEBRUARY

Map your garden, and decide when and where you'll plant each vegetable crop you plan to grow. Keep **adding kitchen scraps** to your **compost pile**, even though you may have to trudge through the snow to do it. Near the end of the month, start spring broccoli and cabbage **seedlings** indoors.

MARCH

Start **preparing beds** by working compost into the soil as soon as the ground has thawed and dried. Start **pepper seedlings** eight weeks before your last frost date; start tomato and eggplant seedlings six weeks before your last frost date. **Plant pea seeds** directly in the garden near the middle of the month if the weather cooperates.

APRIL

Now that the weather is warmer, you can do a lot in the garden, such as:

- **Plant seed potatoes**, and plant lettuce, spinach, and mesclun seed directly in the ground.

- **Plant radish, carrot, and beet seeds** as well as onion sets and shallots.

- Near the end of the month, **plant those broccoli and cabbage seedlings** that you started last month in your garden.

Winter   **Spring**   **Summer**   **Fall**

- Make sure to **mulch your beds**, or you'll spend the next five months or so weeding.

MAY

 If you haven't started your own tomato and pepper seedlings, **buy some transplants** and plant them in the garden after the soil has warmed up. **Place collars** around the transplants' stems for protection against cutworm pests. Also **plant snap beans, corn, squash, and cucumber seeds** directly in your beds.

JUNE

 It's high season in the garden. Now you can:

- **Harvest the peas** (try not to eat all of them before you make it out of the garden!).
- **Harvest salad greens** such as lettuce, spinach, and mesclun before the weather gets too warm and they bolt (go to seed).
- **Pull out weeds** that crop up through your mulch.

- Give your beds plenty of **water** so they stay nice and moist, especially if Mother Nature isn't cooperating.

JULY

 Start **giving away extra zucchini**. Continue watering during dry spells. Harvest onions, snap beans, summer squash, cucumbers, carrots, beets, and the first tomatoes. **Pull out spring crops** that are finished producing for the season, such as peas, lettuce, and broccoli. Throw the spent plants on your compost pile.

AUGUST

 Can tomatoes and continue **harvesting corn**, peppers, snap beans, and the rest of your garden veggies. Plant a **cover crop** in any garden beds that are now empty. Sit in the shade and **relax** with a cold glass of lemonade.

SEPTEMBER

 Can more tomatoes and **make salsa**. Harvest **pumpkins**, carrots, and

beets, and **plant garlic** for next year's crop. Pull more spent plants out of your beds, and continue planting cover crops in empty spaces.

OCTOBER

 Harvest the last of the tomatoes and peppers before the first fall frost. Pull all remaining spent plants out of the beds and plant cover crops. **Collect stakes**, temporary trellises, and row covers, and scrape off clinging soil. **Carve a pumpkin** or two for Halloween.

NOVEMBER

 Rake up leaves and add them to your **compost** pile. **Organize** any notes you took from the gardening season and compile them in a binder, along with a map of what grew where.

DECEMBER

 Relax and enjoy some of those tomatoes you canned back in August and September. Watch the snow fly and dream about next year's garden.

Vegetable Garden Glossary

Learning the lingo that goes with vegetable gardening will make your trips to the home and garden center much easier. Here's a list of terms you're likely to come across in this book, as well as in the gardening aisles.

Beneficials. Helpful creatures, such as birds, bats, toads, snakes, spiders, and predatory insects, that eat pests in the garden.

Bloodmeal. Also known as dried blood, it's a slaughterhouse by-product that contains 13 percent nitrogen. Can be sprinkled on garden beds to repel rabbits.

Bolt. To go to seed. Lettuce, for example, will bolt, or go to seed, when the weather gets too hot.

Bonemeal. Finely ground bones (a by-product of animal slaughterhouses) that contain 10 to 12 percent phosphorus, 24 percent calcium, and a small amount of nitrogen.

Broadcast. To spread fertilizer evenly across an area by hand or with a spreading tool.

BT (*Bacillus thuringiensis*). A spray derived from a naturally occurring bacteria that kills certain insect larvae.

BTK. A BT variety (*BT* var. *kurstaki*) that controls cabbage loopers, cabbageworms, tomato hornworms, fruitworms, European corn borers, and pest larvae.

Cloche. Light-permeable plant covers made out of a variety of materials that are primarily used to protect plants from frost. They work much like miniature greenhouses.

Companion planting. Combinations of plants that work well together to repel pests, attract beneficial insects, or make efficient use of garden beds.

Compost. Decomposed and partially decomposed organic matter (such as kitchen scraps, leaves, grass clippings, and dead plants) that is dark in color and crumbly in texture. Used as an amendment, compost increases the water-holding capacity of the soil and is an excellent nutrient source for microorganisms, which later release nutrients to your plants.

Composting. The art and science of combining organic material so that the original raw ingredients are transformed into compost.

Compost tea. A fertilizer made by soaking a cloth bag full of compost in a watering can or barrel for several days.

Crop rotation. Rotating crops from different botanical families to avoid or reduce problems with soilborne disease or soil insects.

Cover crops. Also called green manures. A crop you plant in an empty bed that will grow rapidly and blanket the soil. Cover crops are used to hold soil in place and provide nutrients over the winter, between plantings of vegetables or between growing seasons, or as a way to rejuvenate poor soil. These crops are either harvested or tilled under into the soil. Examples of cover crops include annual ryegrass, buckwheat, and white clover.

Direct seeding. Planting seeds outside directly into the garden.

Double-digging. The process of removing a shovel full of topsoil from a garden bed, loosening the soil below, and then replacing the topsoil layer for a fertile, productive bed.

Fertilizers. A natural or manufactured material added to the soil that supplies one or more of the major nutrients—nitrogen (N), phosphorus (P), and potassium (K)—to growing plants.

Fish emulsion. Made from filtered fish solubles, fish emulsion contains about 5 percent nitrogen. It's useful for spraying as a foliar feeding spray and to fertilize transplants.

Foliar feed. To supply nutrients by spraying liquid fertilizer directly on plant foliage.

Hardening off. Gradually exposing tender seedlings to the outdoors in a protected area for a week prior to transplanting them into the garden.

Herbicide. Substances used to kill unwanted plants. Some types are selective (they kill only a certain type of plant); others are non-selective and will kill any plants they come into contact with.

Humus. A dark-color, stable form of organic matter that remains after most of the plant and animal residues in it have decomposed.

Mesclun. A mix of salad greens such as endive, arugula, chervil, and lettuce.

NPK ratio. A recognized abbreviation that refers to the ratio of the three major nutrients—nitrogen (N), phosphorus (P), and potassium (K)—in fertilizer, such as 5-5-5 or 10-2-2.

Organic. Materials that are derived directly from plants or animals. Organic gardening uses plant and animal by-products to maintain soil and plant health, and doesn't rely on synthetically made fertilizers, herbicides, or pesticides.

Pesticide. Any substance, synthetic or natural, that is used to kill insects, animals, fungi, bacteria, or weeds.

Raised beds. Three- to five-foot-wide (on average) beds that are higher than ground level and separated by paths. Raised beds increase soil aeration and drainage and save space.

Row covers. Sheets of lightweight, permeable material, usually polypropylene or polyester, that can be laid loosely on top of plants to act as a barrier against insect pests or that can give a few degrees of frost protection at the beginning or end of the growing season.

Seed germination. The beginning of the growth of a seed.

Seedling. A young plant grown from seed. Commonly, plants grown from seeds are termed seedlings until they are first transplanted.

Sidedress. To apply solid (as opposed to liquid) fertilizer alongside annual plants during the growing season.

Soil test kit. A set of instructions and a soil bag available through your state's Cooperative Extension Service. Test results indicate soil pH and specify which amendments and nutrients should be added to your soil.

Wallo'Water. A cloche made of upright, narrow plastic tubes filled with water that can protect tomato and other seedlings from frost.

Recommended Reading & Resources

Books & Periodicals

Bradley, Fern Marshall, and Barbara W. Ellis, eds. *Rodale's All-New Encyclopedia of Organic Gardening*. Emmaus, PA: Rodale, 1992.

Coleman, Eliot. *The New Organic Grower: A Master's Manual of Tools and Techniques for the Home and Market Gardener*. 2nd ed. White River Junction, VT: Chelsea Green, 1995.

Cutler, Karan Davis. *The Complete Vegetable & Herb Gardener: A Guide to Growing Your Garden Organically*. New York: Macmillan, 1997.

Ellis, Barbara W., and Fern Marshall Bradley. *The Organic Gardener's Handbook of Natural Insect and Disease Control*. Emmaus, PA: Rodale, 1992.

Nick, Jean M. A., and Fern Marshall Bradley. *Growing Fruits & Vegetables Organically*. Emmaus, PA: Rodale, 1994.

Ogden, Shepherd. *Step by Step Organic Vegetable Gardening: The Gardening Classic Revised and Updated*. New York: Harper-Collins, 1992.

Organic Gardening Magazine, Rodale Inc., 33 E. Minor Street, Emmaus, PA 18098

Tools & Supplies

Bountiful Gardens
18001 Shafer Ranch Road
Willits, CA 95490
Phone/fax: (707) 459-6410
Web site: www.zapcom.net/~bountiful

The Cook's Garden
P.O. Box 535
Londonderry, VT 05148
Phone: (800) 457-9703
Fax: (800) 457-9705
Web site: www.cooksgarden.com

Gardener's Supply Company
128 Intervale Road
Burlington, VT 05401
Phone: (800) 863-1700
Fax: (800) 551-6712
Web site: www.gardeners.com

Gardens Alive!
5100 Schenley Place
Lawrenceburg, IN 47025
Phone: (812) 537-8650
Fax: (812) 537-5108
Web site: www.gardens-alive.com

Johnny's Selected Seeds
Foss Hill Road
Albion, ME 04910
Phone: (207) 437-4357
Fax: (800) 437-4290 (U.S. only)
Fax: (207) 437-2165 (outside continental U.S.)
Web site: www.johnnyseeds.com

Native Seeds/SEARCH
526 North 4th Avenue
Tucson, AZ 85705-8450
Phone: (520) 622-5561
Fax: (520) 622-5591
Web site: www.azstarnet.com/~nss

Park Seed
1 Parkton Avenue
Greenwood, SC 29647-0001
Phone: (800) 845-3369
Fax: (800) 275-9941
Web site: www.parkseed.com

Peaceful Valley Farm Supply
P.O. Box 2209
Grass Valley, CA 95945
Phone: (530) 272-4769
Fax: (530) 272-4794
Web site: www.groworganic.com

Seeds Blüm
27 Idaho City Stage Road
Boise, ID 83716
Phone: (800) 742-1423
Fax: (208) 338-5658
Web site: www.seedsblum.com

Shepherd's Garden Seeds
30 Irene Street
Torrington, CT 06790-6658
Phone: (860) 482-3638
Fax: (860) 482-0532
Web site: www.shepherdseeds.com

W. Atlee Burpee Company
300 Park Avenue
Warminster, PA 18974
Phone: (800) 888-1447
Fax: (800) 487-5530
Web site: www.burpee.com

Acknowledgments

Contributors to this book include Jill Jesiolowski Cebenko, Lois Trigg Chaplan, Barbara Ellis, Cheryl Long, Vicki Mattern, Scott Meyer, Jean Nick, Barbara Pleasant, and Joanna Poncavage.

Photo Credits

William Adams 2, 29

Rob Cardillo 4, 8, 9, 14, 22, 31, 59, 70, 72, 74, 76, 77, 87, 89, 94, 95

Christi Carter/Grant Heilman Photography 16

David Cavagnaro 42, 66

Walter Chandoha 6, 10, 11, 12, 18, 36, 47, 49, 69, 81

Stewart Cohen/Tony Stone Images 38

Crandall and Crandall 58

Robin B. Cushman/Photo Garden, Inc. 56 (top)

Dembinsky Photo Associates 54 (top)

Thomas E. Eltzroth 27

Tony Giammarino 21

Bill Johnson 53 (top), 55 (bottom), 56 (bottom), 61

Kit Latham iv, 34

Lefever-Grushow/Grant Heilman Photography vii

Larry Lefever/Grant Heilman Photography 13

Mitch Mandel 25

Diane A. Pratt 50

Heath Robbins 15

Maria Rodale 41

Rodale Stock Images 78, 82, 84, 85, 86, 90

Runk-Schoenberger/Grant Heilman Photography 55 (top)

Arthur C. Smith III/Grant Heilman Photography 63

Stephen R. Swinburne 64

Ron West 53 (bottom), 54 (bottom)

Rick Wetherbee 20, 24, 32, 39, 45, 80, 93

Index

USDA Plant Hardiness Zone Map

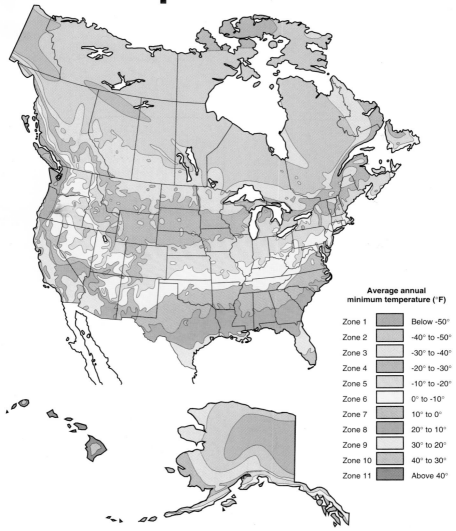

Average annual minimum temperature (°F)

Zone		Temperature
Zone 1		Below -50°
Zone 2		-40° to -50°
Zone 3		-30° to -40°
Zone 4		-20° to -30°
Zone 5		-10° to -20°
Zone 6		0° to -10°
Zone 7		10° to 0°
Zone 8		20° to 10°
Zone 9		30° to 20°
Zone 10		40° to 30°
Zone 11		Above 40°

This map was revised in 1990 and is recognized as the best indicator of minimum temperatures available. Look at the map to find your area, then match its color to the key at the right. When you've found your color, the key will tell you what hardiness zone you live in. Remember that the map is a general guide; your particular conditions may vary.